Marriage and the Bible

Marriage and the Bible

Ernest White

BROADMAN PRESS
Nashville, Tennessee

To
my wife Bonnie
who has lived the ideals
described herein

Usually Scripture references are from the *Revised Standard Version,*
copyright 1946, 1952.

DEWEY DECIMAL CLASSIFICATION: 220.8
Library of Congress catalog card number: 65–15598
Printed in the United States of America
5.N64KSP

Preface

Jesus and his first interpreters answered immediate, pressing questions about marriage and related matters. They left it to each generation to meet the perplexities of its own time, using as guides the absolute ideals and the redemptive attitude of Jesus. Thus a telescopic view is needed at present to demonstrate the relevance of the biblical understanding of marriage for twentieth-century Christian homes. Underlying assumptions which served as bases on which New Testament questions were answered remain solid as foundation stones. But these need to be rediscovered so that they may speak meaningfully to contemporary men and women in the Christian fellowship.

Local environments and foreign cultures influenced the New Testament writers' views of marriage. The honest interpreter, therefore, must recognize and consider these elements. He must effect some value judgments in order to make distinctions between those views which are historically limited and those which are permanently valid. There is, of course, the danger of producing an interpretation which reflects only the interpreter's culture and environment.

The legalist will seek to extract from the New Testament a series of rules which cover the various questions about marriage. It is sufficient with this approach to be able to produce a scriptural quotation, often without reference to its setting or without regard to other scriptural references. Legalism applies its pronouncements to all situations without regard to circumstances, not even the circumstance of the redemption of the persons involved.

Thomas Aquinas, more than any other, has done this in the realm of marriage for the Roman Catholic Church.

Closely related to the legalist approach is the institutional, which is in reality one of the assumptions on which the legalist approach is made. Sociologists, especially, see marriage as an institution of society which must be preserved or protected by laws. In this, marriage is seen as an end in itself and invites the legalist interpretation of the New Testament teaching on marriage. Jesus observed this legalistic mistake about the sabbath, and if we would paraphrase his words, making them refer to marriage, they would say: "Marriage was made for man, and not man for marriage."

The institutional approach sees marriage as almost having an existence and rights without relation to the lives of men and women who live in the married state. The laws enunciated and enacted are established for the preservation of marriage as an institution of society without regard to the interior character of the relationship.

It is, therefore, the concern of this work to view the New Testament teachings about marriage in light of Jesus' relational concept of life. He saw human life, not in terms of laws or institutions, but in terms of personal encounter and relationship. His greatest concern, of course, was man's relationship with God (the Great Commandment). In contrast to the legalism in which the Pharisees viewed this relationship, Jesus looked behind the religious acts of men to uncover the character of their intentions and motives. These, he proclaimed, determined the rightness of divine-human relations. He was not as concerned about whether an offering was brought to the Temple as he was about the relationship one had with others when the gift was presented (cf. Matt. 5:23 ff.).

This same approach is demonstrated in Jesus' view of strictly human relationships. It is not enough physically to abide by the commandment, "You shall not commit adultery." It is imperative that the desire not be cultivated (cf. Matt. 5:27). In the matter of seeking forgiveness, it is the restoration of fellowship that is to be desired, not the satisfaction of the legal number of times to offer forgiveness (cf. Matt. 18:15–22). In a word, the revolt of Jesus against the Pharisees was his reaction to their meticulous legalism. They were cleansing the outside of the cup by minute regulations while inwardly the relationships of life with both God and man were highly infected.

To see marriage primarily as a relationship of both strictly human and divine-human dimensions is the task undertaken here. This will necessitate viewing not only the absolute ideals for marriage but also seeing how these ideals were applied. Jesus and his first followers gave some very practical and redemptive expressions of these ideals. When the ideals are viewed, better understood are the words "Be ye therefore perfect." On the other hand, when the actual applications are made, Jesus' other words are also meaningful as he said, "The Son of man is come to seek and to save that which was lost" (Luke 19:10, KJV).

Much of the inspiration and encouragement for this work have come from three men who challenged me to serious study of the New Testament. They are Drs. Wayne E. Oates, Henry E. Turlington, and Heber F. Peacock. I am grateful also to helpful secretaries and the interested and patient people in the churches where I have served, particularly the Wyatt Park Baptist Church of St. Joseph, Missouri.

Contents

1. The Biblical View of Man

What is man? The wondering query of the psalmist is still being probed. What sort of creature man sees himself to be determines how he will relate to others and to his total environment. Current discussions in the social sciences and theology are discovering some interesting parallels. Two theologians who have taken serious note of these, as well as significant differences, are Wayne E. Oates, *Religious Dimensions of Personality*, and David Cox, *Jung and St. Paul*.

It is imperative at the outset of this discussion to determine as clearly as possible the biblical view of man. If men and women are to relate themselves totally to each other in marital relationship, they must have an adequate concept of the nature of their individual existences. The tendency for persons to see themselves as parts prevents the communication of the total self. Hebrew anthropology provided a sound basis from which to develop a theology of marriage.

The Hebraic Idea of Man

The outstanding characteristic of Hebrew thought with regard to the structure of man is that of unity. This structure is usually termed wholistic and it is at this point that present studies in psychology run parallel. Psychical and physical functions are closely related. Parts of the body are referred to as giving psychical reactions. For example, the psalmist's prayer was worded, "Make me to hear joy and gladness; that the bones which thou hast broken may rejoice" (51:8, KJV).

1

Another linguistic practice of the Hebrews which reveals this wholistic concept of personality was the use of synecdoche (*pars pro toto*). In this way any one part of the body could be referred to as representing the whole in expressing the functions of the personality. There are about eighty such parts which are so used.

The one word which is used most for the whole of man is *basar* (flesh). *Basar* usually stands for the whole life substance of men organized in corporeal form, but there is no one word which is used for the whole of the body as such. Nor does the use of a part for the whole indicate any "partition" view of personality by the Hebrews. The famous sentence of H. Wheeler Robinson is "the Hebrew ideal of personality is an animated body, and not an incarnated soul," and so it is that "man does not *have* a body, he *is* a body." [1]

An emphasis on the theocentric relationship of man is quite evident in Old Testament writings. The life principle which distinguishes man from beast is that which has been given to man by his Creator. The spirit of man was a means of expressing the whole range of man's emotional, intellectual, and relational life. The dynamic of man's personality found its source in and was ultimately responsible to a right relationship to God.

Other words which are used in Hebrew thought for the inner aspects of man's life are *nephesh* (soul or life) and *leb* (heart). In the former of these the translation and understanding of the word as soul in the Greek sense as distinguished from the body is a mistake. Such a division was entirely foreign to the Hebrews. Its use in the Old Testament is adapted to various mental and emotional states, but its most basic meaning is "to denote one's 'person' or 'self' as a center of consciousness and unity of vital power." [2] *Leb* on the other hand is mentioned even more frequently than *nephesh* and refers to the inner emotional and volitional aspect of man's being. All of these terms lend themselves "to expressing the unity of the personality under the various aspects of its fundamental relation to God." [3]

Another striking characteristic of the Hebrew concept of personality is that it is essentially social. *Basar* (flesh) was the word most used to convey this idea in Hebrew language. Human life for the Israelite necessitated horizontal dimensions as well as vertical. This social aspect to a personality led to the concept of corporate personality as expressed through a unity of purpose in a group of people which often included the whole nation of Israel. Neither the individual man nor the nation was conceived in terms of isolated parts. The fate of the nation was the fate of the individual. A man's life and actions affected his family and tribe and even the entire nation. Thus, personality to the Hebrew was one of wholeness before God and in relation to other men. Two New Testament concepts emphasize this wholeness, of which the first is translated flesh.

Flesh

The words for flesh in Hebrew and Greek produce a whole spectrum of meanings. *Basar,* the Hebrew word, begins with the same meaning as the English word "flesh" in standing for the soft muscular portions of a body, but it can also suggest "by synecdoche" the whole body. To this usage in particular we shall return at the latter part of this discussion.

On the basis of the fact of flesh producing natural generation, *basar* is sometimes used to denote one's kindred. In the Old Testament there is very little, if any, use of flesh to specify a power for evil. There is the suggestion of inherent weakness and frailty in *basar* but it is physical and not ethical.

Sarx (flesh), like the Hebrew *basar*, has as its basic meaning the flesh substance of man and beast. Thus in classical writings it was always used in a purely physical sense and referred to the material out of which the body was made. Not simply in the New Testament but by that time, and especially among New Testament writers, *sarx* became a highly developed term. One of the steps taken was the use of *sarx* to denote the exterior being of man in his specific humanness. It could represent all that came to a man by reason of heredity (cf. Phil. 3:4).

There was a usage where *sarx* meant man in general and especially marked off human life in contrast to divine being (cf. 1 Cor. 1:29; Rom. 3:20).

This contrast to divine being emphasized the weakness and inability of human life, so that flesh bears also the connotation of human infirmity.

Nor is the *sarx* simply a part of the person; rather it is the whole body or the whole person in his external physical existence. Therefore, the *sarx* is not the material out of which a *soma* (body) is formed; the *sarx* is the *soma* (body). It is possible thus to use *sarx* as the designation for the person himself as, for example, in 2 Corinthians 7:5, where "our *sarx*" is translated, "I found no rest." This identification is made again in Ephesians 5:29, in reference to marriage where "his own flesh" is equal to "himself." This connotation of *sarx* as a representation of the whole person is especially relevant for an understanding of marriage. It not only emphasizes that the totality of personality and being is invested in the marriage relationship, but the concept of "one flesh" is the basic description of the marriage relationship. Here two personalities become one flesh and find the fulfilment of their being in that relationship.

There is yet a further development in the concept of *sarx* which grew out of the idea of inherent weakness in the flesh. The physical infirmity of which we have spoken is accompanied, in the writings of Paul and other New Testament writers, by an ethical weakness which emphasizes the sinfulness of man. This usage does not mean that as material the flesh is sinful; it is not a Greek dualism. Rather, it is the fact that *sarx* represents the entire sphere of man's earthly nature. It becomes the vehicle which expresses his sinfulness.

When *sarx* is described as sinful, it is understood as man living for the world, not as man living in the world. In this ethical sense *sarx* is a power which takes hold of man and determines him. Several phrases are used in the New Testament to convey the varying degrees of this ethical weakness. The phrase "in the flesh" is sometimes used to mean under the power of sin (Rom. 8:8–9), and at other times it is simply a designation of earthly, human life (cf. Phil. 1:24).

"Fleshly" is used to describe wisdom and desires which are confined to earthly, human life in contrast to that which comes from God (cf. 2 Cor. 1:12; 1 Peter 2:11). One of the favorite phrases of the apostle Paul was "according to the flesh." By this he meant both that which is the result of natural generation (cf. Rom. 1:3) and that which is confined to earthly existence, completely separated from any consideration of spiritual dimensions.

This pursuit of life "according to the flesh" stands in rebellion against God.

The other phrase which accompanies "according to the flesh" and lends it distinctiveness is "according to the spirit." The ethical and moral weakness of *sarx* is emphasized in this contrast with spirit (*pneuma*). Thus it is not that sin inheres in the flesh as material; rather, in flesh there is a pursuit of life which excludes the spiritual pursuit. The contrast is made especially clear in Romans 8 in the list of the fruits of the flesh. In Galatians 5:19–21, the activities and attitudes described are not simply those which have to do with satisfaction of the physical body; instead many of them relate to the direction of personality and the defiance of spiritual leadership in one's life. *Sarx*, especially for Paul, becomes the base from which sin assails man.

While it may seem that this use of *sarx* to denote ethical and moral rebellion against God stands at the opposite pole from its use as a representation of the whole personality of man, the proximity is closer than first appears. In reality this latter usage is also a description of the personality of man perverted in its relationship both to God and to man himself. Later it will become clear that this perverted relationship can exist not only with the individual but also in the one-flesh concept. The will of God is directed toward both the redemption of *sarx* of the individual and the redemption of one flesh in marriage. Some usages of *sarx* and the *soma* concept, discussed next, parallel closely.

The Soma Concept

Like the *sarx* concept, *soma* (body) in the New Testament is based on the extensive Hebrew concept of *basar* (flesh). It should be noted again that the Hebrews did not have a word for body as such but used parts to stand for the whole. While Greek philosophical writers used *soma* to distinguish between body and soul or spirit, New Testament writers, especially Paul, maintained the concept of man as a whole and *soma* as an expression of the whole. Similar also to *sarx*, *soma* can be used as the equivalent of the personal pronoun, e.g., "Christ will be honored in my body [in me], whether by life or by death" (Phil. 1:20).

Externality is the aspect of man's being which is emphasized by the use of *soma*. This is not meant in a dualistic sense, whereby the body is simply the form or shell which houses the soul; rather, it is the self objectified. As a body (*soma*), man is able to make himself the object of his own thinking and acting. In his somatic existence, he bears a relationship to himself and is able to enter into relationships of life.

There is always the possibility that the relationship man bears may be a perverted one if he is not rightly related to God. Man receives and responds to life's experiences (most of which come to him through his body) by means of this somatic externality, through which he expresses the various reactions in the factors of his personality. Thus, the *soma* is in reality the vehicle of expression for the personality.

Much of the foregoing description of *soma* (body) runs parallel to the previous discussion of *sarx* (flesh), making it appear that there is little if any difference between the two concepts. The identification is actually made in Colossians 2:11: "by putting off the body (*soma*) of flesh (*sarx*) in the circumcision of Christ." Either of the words here could have been dropped with little loss of concept. Yet the identification is not complete. J. A. T. Robinson points out, "While *sarx* stands for man in the solidarity of creation in his distance from God, *soma* stands for man in the solidarity of creation as made for God." [4]

Further differences appear in Paul's use of *soma* in discussions of the future life (cf. 1 Cor. 15:44). He conceives a body which is not mortal, transitory, nor corruptible. The idea is implied that the heavenly *soma* would not be of flesh. This suggests another difference in that here as elsewhere *soma*, unlike *sarx*, does not connote weakness and mortality. Somatic existence is the only kind of existence which is conceived in the New Testament, whether upon earth or in heaven. Man is a *soma*; he does not merely have a *soma*.

Paul draws parallels between man as a *soma* and the church as a *soma*. In this aspect of his being, man as a *soma* is an organized and functioning self. When he is rightly related within himself as *soma*, there is harmony in his functioning and each part or member finds its meaning and purpose in its relation to the whole. Here again, the emphasis is placed upon the whole. This analogy applied to the church reminds believers that as such their functions and abilities are bound up in the proper functioning of the whole church. Believers in Christ are not to exist independently or separately from others and the church; rather, they find the meaning of their existence in their relation to the whole. For one such member to extricate himself from the functioning of the rest is to destroy the right relation of the entire *soma* (cf. 1 Cor. 12; Rom. 12).

In identifying believers as the temple of God, the apostle uses both the personal pronoun and *soma*. The Corinthians are reminded, "Do you not know that you are God's temple and God's Spirit dwells in you?" (1 Cor. 3:16). Later comes another exhortation, "We are the temple of the living God" (2 Cor. 6:16). Between these two he has occasion to admonish them about sexual license and asks, "Do you not know that your body is a temple of the Holy Spirit within you, which you have from God?" (1 Cor. 6:19). There can be little question here but that *soma* is used to denote man's whole personality in his relationship to God. Man is related to God as a whole being; he is to be redeemed not just as a soul separated from the body but as a *soma*, which includes all—"soul and body." When man is redeemed as a whole person his relationships in every direction are corrected and he becomes the dwelling place for the Spirit of God.

Sexuality in Relation to Soma

Sexual power is conceived in the New Testament as power of the *soma*. The apostle Paul reflects this in his statement about Abraham, "He did not weaken in faith when he considered his own body, which was as good as dead" (Rom. 4:19). Not only is the *soma* the carrier of sexual power, it is the seat or source of sexual power. Illustrative of this fact is the New Testament attitude toward sexual sins as sins of the *soma*. Homosexuality is described by Paul as "the dishonoring of their bodies" (Rom. 1:24). In dealing with a case of prostitution, he begins his reasoning against it by stating, "The body is not meant for immorality" (1 Cor. 6:13). Later he states the principle, "Every other sin which a man commits is outside the body; but the immoral man sins against his own body" (v. 18). Immorality or unchastity, then, is considered a perversion of the relationship which man bears within himself because it attempts to separate sexuality from the rest of personality. Such a separation and "using" of the personality destroys man as a whole being.

It is not possible to separate a person from his sexuality; the sexual desires of a person are the expressions of the self. Since the *soma* is the source and carrier of sexual power, it is not simply the flesh which has sexual desires but the self. The sexuality of a man is an integral aspect of his total personality. In the phrase and its counterpart, "The wife does not rule over her own body, but the husband does" (1 Cor. 7:4), it is implied that in sexual union the total self is surrendered. As noted above, the Old Testament writers used various parts, e.g., sexual and reproductive organs, such as loins and womb, to denote by synecdoche the body and personality as a whole. The reference to the adulterous union in 1 Corinthians 6:13–20 indicates that sexual union reaches the very core of man's being. Thus, sexual functioning is, by the very nature of man, the entering of the whole personality into the relationship established.

Sexuality in Creation

In considering the nature of man it is imperative to grasp the biblical view that sexuality in man is an intended and basic element in creation. This point is the anthropological groundwork for a theology of sex. The fact of creation by male and female and the biblical concept that all creation, including human bisexuality, was good allowed the Hebrews a very positive approach to sexual matters. This aspect of creation, of course, is shared by other animals and much of the rest of living creation, but the differences between man and the rest of creation gives sexuality in man a significance not present elsewhere. For this reason, a simple argument from animal nature does not suffice to establish meaning or morality for human sexuality.

Plato's sexual-creation story emphasizes the idea of one sex completing the other, but in quite a different manner than the Hebrews' account. In his account, bisexuality was the result of vengeance in which Androgynes was split so that sexuality of one gender represents only half of original man. Quite a different view of sex is given in the Genesis account, where bisexuality was an intended and purposeful arrangement of the Creator. The Hebrew originals for male and female emphasize in their derivations the sexual aspect of creation. Otto Piper observes in a comparison of the two ideas, "With him [Plato] the sexual relationship was merely instrumental in discovering the true partner; it had no dignity in itself." [5] The contrast between the Hebrew and Greek concepts of sexuality grew sharper as later Greek philosophers sought escape from the body and its functions.

In this chapter we have attempted to survey some of the main points of biblical anthropology. The Hebraic concept of personality which emphasizes its wholeness runs through both the Old and New Testaments. However, the New Testament terms like *sarx* and *soma* need to be understood in the Hebrew tradition rather than in their Greek meaning or in their English translations.

The similarities and differences in the connotations of *sarx* and *soma* help us to understand Paul's wide use of both terms. It is important to know that while *sarx* is the vehicle which often expresses sin, it is not in and of itself sinful. Its moral weakness inheres in the fact that sin permeates the whole of man's personality and the flesh becomes the expression of the infection.

No other existence was conceived for man than that of a *soma*. While *soma* denoted man in organized form, it was not confined to form. Man as *soma* is also man having a relationship to himself and entering into relationships with others, especially God. With our concern for marriage and its expressions here, attention has been called to the *soma* as the source and carrier of sexual power and in return the idea that sexual activity as sin is activity or sin of the body and whole self.

This complete association of sex and *soma* stems from the fact of sexuality as a basic and intended aspect of creation. Sexuality hereby is the self, functioning and giving expression to the personality. It remains for us to consider further the relation of sexuality to personality and discover its true purposes. To this pursuit we now turn.

2. Sexuality as God's Creation

The Greeks had no word for sex as such; nor did the Hebrews. However, there was a Greek word to denote the act of sexual intercourse which related it to its place of occurrence. Thus the word *koite* actually meant a bed (cf. Luke 11:7) but meant sexual intercourse, both honorable (cf. Heb. 13:4) and illicit (cf. Rom. 13:13). Still this did not mean that the Greeks or Hebrews were reticent to discuss sexual matters, for they did so freely and chose words or phrases for precise and vivid description.

Reference has already been made to the Hebrew view of sexuality but here we shall consider it further to attempt to assess the true nature of human sexuality, including its purposes and functions. Seward Hiltner makes the observation, "In its human form, sex is like human freedom itself—responsible alike for man's highest achievements and for his greatest sins." [1] The appropriateness of this observation is uncovered through the statements and attitudes displayed in the New Testament.

Otto Piper has given good expression to a Christian concept of sexuality. He gives two very fine analyses of sexuality in the Bible. The first he calls "the main points in this biblical understanding of sex." The points he lists are: (1) the essentially complementary character of man and woman; (2) the essential difference of the sexes; (3) the change of nature called forth by sexual intercourse." [2] Later he gives "five ideas fundamental to the biblical interpretation of sex. These are: (1) In sexual intercourse two persons of different sex become joined in an indissoluble unity; (2) sex is meaningful in itself, creating a specific kind of personal relationship; (3) in sex life one attains knowledge of the inner secret of one's own physical being; (4) in love sustained by faith sex attains its consummation and perfection; (5) sex life is necessary and good but not absolutely essential for a full human life." [3]

In these analyses, Piper has set forth the goals of our understanding which we will seek to examine in the following pages.

The Nature of Sexuality

Both from the Hebrew concept, found in the creation account, and the above understanding of the nature of man, sexuality is looked upon as basically good. References in the New Testament support this view, such as the exhortation to "let the marriage bed be undefiled." The pastoral injunction against asceticism and the accompanying statement that sex should be received as a gift from God also gives strength to positive acceptance: "Who forbid marriage . . . which God created to be received with thanksgiving by those who believe and know the truth. For everything created by God is good" (1 Tim. 4:3–4).

An asceticism which seeks salvation or virtue in itself is unbiblical and unchristian. Denial of sexuality as a good in itself is a refusal of God's creation and intention for human life. Reasons for celibacy are to be considered at a later time in this work, but not as a means to salvation. The exaltation of celibacy or asceticism as a superior life is based on a Greek concept of the body as a prison house of the soul and celibacy as the open window of escape for the soul. In this there is not only a denial of sexuality as good by virtue of creation but man is split up into compartments of body and soul, with no total view of personality.

Knowledge and sexuality dwell in close connection in biblical writings. The use of "to know" to mean sexual intercourse was more than a Hebrew desire to avoid discussion of delicate matters; rather, it is a revelation of an attitude toward the meaning of sexuality.

Paul Haupt has established the connection between "to know" and "to have sexual commerce." [4] Beginning with the Assyrian equivalent of the Hebrew *yada* (to know) of which the primary connotation is "to smell," he shows that this has come to mean "to perceive through the nose" or "by minute investigation"; thus "to learn" or "to know thoroughly."

Bauman, before Haupt, stated that sexual intercourse originally meant "to acknowledge" or "to care for." Haupt establishes another connection between knowledge and the reproductive system by showing the kinship of Greek *gignoskein,* "to know," and *gignesthai,* "to be born." Further evidence of etymological connection is found in the use of Hebrew *moyda* (which comes from *yada*) to mean, not "acquaintance," but "relation" or "relative."

Paul Haupt introduces also the idea that there is a correspondence between the time a child discerns right and wrong and the time of pubescence, thus an indication of the connection between knowledge and sexuality. There was assumed a correspondence between the age of consent to marry and the ability to consummate marriage. These, then, are the bases for the biblical use of "to know" to connote sexual intercourse.

The indiscriminate use of "to know" in the Bible for all kinds of sexual relations takes cognizance of the fact that sexuality can become the means of communication for deep and unutterable knowledge between persons. Piper characterizes the knowledge gained by sexual experience in three points: "(a) It is strictly personal knowledge; (b) its subject matter consists in the mutual relationship between two parties; (c) it is knowledge of an inner secret." [5] The mutual self-disclosure of sexual intercourse is of the nature whereby the individual becomes aware of the meaning of being male or female. In sexual intercourse one discovers the meaning of one's own existence while discovering the personal being of the other individual to which one is thus joined.

An understanding of the knowledge involved in sex leads to a consideration of the radical nature of sexuality, for knowledge that is imparted in sexual intercourse cannot be erased. Therefore, the participating individuals can never return to their former state. They are, in a measure, permanently and inseparably bound together by the knowledge which they have gained of themselves and of one another in the experience. Without explaining in detail the process, Jesus assumed this in his statement of the original intention for marriage: "But from the beginning of creation, 'God made them male and female.' For this reason a man shall leave his father and mother and be joined to his wife, and the two shall become one [flesh]. So they are no longer two but one" (Mark 10:6–8).

Thus the radical nature of sex involves the establishment of one flesh. The apostle Paul reveals understanding of the accomplishment of "one flesh" by his remarks in reference to an illicit union: "Do you not know that he who joins himself to a prostitute becomes one body with her? For, as it is written, 'The two shall become one [flesh]' " (1 Cor. 6:16). Here it is shown that sexual intercourse establishes one flesh and that this is true even when the relationship is a perverted one, such as that to which Paul refers. This does not mean that the sex act comprises the whole of the one-flesh concept, but it is the *basic symbol*. In this we are led to one of the most basic purposes of sexuality.

The Purposes and Functions of Sexuality

At least four purposes of sexuality introduce themselves in a careful review of the treatment of marriage in the New Testament. The first of these made its entrance in the foregoing discussion of the radical nature of sex. Quite certainly the establishment of one flesh in the marriage relationship is one of the foremost purposes of human sexuality. The fact that it has received so little attention has been due to an underestimation of the one-flesh concept and an overemphasis on marriage as an institution for producing children. More than any other, the one-flesh idea allows marriage to be seen primarily for what it is—namely, a *relationship*.

Beginning with the fuller understandings of the terms *sarx* and *soma*, arrived at in the discussion of man's nature, we have the framework for understanding one flesh. We have seen that these refer not simply to part of man but to his entire personality. The establishment of one flesh in marriage is the establishment of an irrevocable unity by two total personalities. Paul understood that sexual union is the symbol of this unity in his reference to a perverted relationship already noticed in 1 Corinthians 6:16.

Validation for sexual union as the symbol of one flesh is found in the expressiveness and comprehensiveness of sexuality. The entire person is given to another in sexual union as expressed by the apostle's reminder, "The wife does not rule over her own body, but the husband does; likewise the husband does not rule over his own body, but the wife does" (1 Cor. 7:4). The fact that the total self is surrendered in intercourse renders any attempt to do less a perversion of sexuality. Symbolically and effectively sexuality becomes a vehicle of the total person in marriage.

Not only in its comprehensiveness, but in its intensity as well, the sexual union is effective in establishing one flesh. That aspect of the flesh or personality which expresses the inmost being of the person is sexuality. Hence we have noted that the biblical language for *knowledge* and *to know* is appropriate for sexual union and connotes its interior character.

Sexual union is the deepest and most potentially meaningful of human interpersonal relationships. The relationship establishes a mutual knowledge and dependency from which there can be no satisfactory return. Therefore, this relationship can be looked upon as neither temporary nor external, but one which demands a life permanency. Reuel Howe understands the meaning of sexual union as "the great gift of God to man . . . the woman and man in married love may come together freely and unashamedly in the communion of the flesh and spirit in the experience of re-creation." [6]

It is particularly to be noted that in the New Testament the emphasis is not upon the dictum "be fruitful and multiply" but rather "the two shall become one flesh." Establishment and maintenance of this personal relationship receives prominent attention throughout the New Testament in sexual matters. Procreation is not denied; it is just tacitly assumed and receives no consideration. Jesus himself pointed back to the one-flesh relationship as marriage. Paul gives primary attention to the acceptability of the relationship in his advice to the Corinthians (cf. 1 Cor. 7:3–5). D. S. Bailey says of the intention of this passage: "Life as 'one-flesh' means surrender of one's body to the other, in return for which one receives the responsibility of 'power' over the other's body." [7]

The mutual exchange of bodily control and love in Ephesians (5:28–31) has as its basis the one-flesh quotation from the Old Testament. Consideration by the husband is based upon a correct personal relationship as it is advised in 1 Peter 3:7, "Likewise you husbands, live considerately with your wives, bestowing honor on the woman as the weaker sex." Either implicitly or explicitly nearly all the relevant New Testament passages present the relationship as basic in marriage, and most of these put it in terms of one flesh. Hence, the enhancement and expression of this relationship gives sexuality a primary place in marriage.

A less obvious but no less real purpose of sexuality in marriage is the fulfilment of the personality in sexual union. This aspect of sexuality is implied in the preceding discussion of one flesh but deserves amplification. Plato, in his concept of the splitting of Androgynes, lays hold of the idea of fulfilment of the incomplete person in sexual union. Whereas, his concept is based on the caprice of the gods, the biblical presentation ascribes divine wisdom and goodness as the basis for sexual creation. The implication of bisexual creation, accepted by Jesus as right and good, is that both the male personality and the female personality find their meaning in sexual union. Personality, which has sexuality as one of its factors, is enhanced and developed by proper sexual functioning.

Proper sexual desires may, therefore, be looked upon as a drive for completion of the individuals involved. The reunion achieved is a kind of redemption for persons who would otherwise be incomplete by themselves. Personal existence as well as masculinity or femininity comes to have new meaning in sexual union. In this vein it is right to speak, as Reuel Howe does, of sexual union as the "instrument for the realization of fullness of being." Sylvanus Duvall sums up this aspect of sexuality in saying, "Sex is to be properly understood and evaluated, only in terms of its contributions to personal fulfillment and ultimate purposes of God." [8]

The next logical consideration with regard to sexuality is its effect upon the spiritual life of man. If sexuality is included in the good creation of God in man and expressive of the whole person, proper sexual functioning can be to the glory of God in the body. Hence, one of the purposes of sexuality is the sanctification of the individual. In fact, the very nature of sexual functioning in its prescribed limits is illustrative of the meaning of sanctification, whereby the person is set aside to the purposes of God. Seward Hiltner suggests that God is glorified in this way: "Through the mystery of sex, God is revealed in the same process by which the depth of another, and consequently one's self, is revealed in a new way." [9]

In order for sex to be an instrument of sanctification for the person, sexuality must be exercised in *agape* (Christian love). Where sexual intercourse between husband and wife is a relationship not simply with each other but also one which is bound up in their grace experience with Christ, it is possible for the Spirit to dwell in their lives so that this gift of love is an opportunity for salvation and sanctification. When *agape* is operative the marriage partners do not look upon each other as a sexual thing but as a person, and in this way it is understandable that "husbands should love their wives as their own bodies."

Sexuality as a means of sanctification of the body must assume its proper proportions as an aspect of personality. Jesus and Paul demonstrated that while sex is a necessary and good arrangement of ordering human life in this world, it must be subservient to the will of God for one's life and preparation for future life. In some cases this might mean celibacy (cf. Matt. 19:10–12; 1 Cor. 7:17).

A striking facet of this thought of sanctification is the sanctification of an unbelieving spouse by a believing partner: "The unbelieving husband is consecrated through his wife, and the unbelieving wife is consecrated through her husband. Otherwise, your children would be unclean, but as it is they are holy" (1 Cor. 7:14).

Piper seeks to explain this by saying: "We have already seen, indeed, how much the sex life of one partner depends on the way in which he is met. Hence, by an inner necessity, the sanctification of one spouse leads to a transformation of the sex life of the other." [10]

However, there is another idea here quite in keeping with Paul's background in the concept of believers making up a new Israel. The Levitical code provided that a child born of the union of an Israelite and a non-Israelite was legitimate in the sense of being an accepted member of the Israelite race (cf. Yeb. 11:2). Carrying over this idea, Paul is assuring his readers that the union of a believer and an unbeliever is valid and that children born of such a union are not, in that sense, illegitimate. Therefore, if any were contemplating leaving an unbelieving spouse on that ground, it was unnecessary. It is the believer who thus "sanctifies" the unbeliever to the point that the union and the children born of the union are not sinful. This point establishes the validity of the union, not the salvation of the unbelieving spouse.

Peter recommends a formula for the actual salvation of an unbelieving partner by telling the wives, "Be submissive to your husbands, so that some, though they do not obey the word, may be won without a word by the behavior of their wives, when they see your reverent and chaste behavior" (1 Peter 3:1–2). A life of such understanding and consideration that would compel an unbeliever to faith certainly would be one that was being sanctified in the marriage relationship; i.e., serving the purposes of God. This, of course, would include far more than the sexual relationship, but would require compatibility and a Christian spirit.

One of the important purposes assigned to sex in the Old Testament is that of procreation, so a prodigious marriage was looked upon as a great blessing. However, this was neither the exclusive nor primary emphasis in sexual matters even in the Old Testament. Of equal concern is the emphasis upon the relational aspect of sex as found in the one-flesh concept and the fidelity required in the Yahweh-Israel marriage figure.

There is no denial in the New Testament of the purpose of procreation. The subject is practically ignored. As shown above, the emphasis is almost entirely on the relational aspect of marriage. The procreative purpose appears to be tacitly assumed and accepted without elaboration. The inference may be drawn that a proper sexual union was expected to be fruitful but not to the exclusion of other purposes and functions in sexual relationship. Certainly there is no indication as to the degree of fruitfulness that is expected. In fact, due to the eschatological cloud which lingers over New Testament thought, there is a degree of abhorrence of childbearing (cf. Mark 13:17 and parallels).

Roman Catholic theologians, passing along statements from men like Augustine and Thomas Aquinas, have claimed primacy for the procreative purpose because these earlier theologians made it the exclusive purpose. E. C. Messenger expresses the Catholic position by saying: "So far, we have been considering only the primary end of sexual intercourse, i.e., the reproduction of the species. But, especially in man, the sexual act has other 'secondary' ends, and in particular, it constitutes an eminently natural expression of the mutual love of husband and wife for each other." [11] He describes the recent trends of Roman Catholic theology thus:

Modern theologians, in contrast to medieval ones, teach that the sex act is lawful and good if performed for one of the recognized secondary ends, such as the expressing of mutual love, the abating of concupiscence, the rendering of the marriage debt, etc., provided the primary end of the act is not positively excluded by the performers. It need not be positively willed. But the positive exclusion of the primary end makes the performance of the act sinful.[12]

Hence, even in Roman Catholic theology, other purposes and functions of sexuality are being recognized. In the main, however, Roman Catholic theology has ignored the deeper meaning of one flesh and the personality fulfilment factor. It has been thus seemingly unconscious of the relational aspect of sexual union. The general celibacy of Catholic theologians may account for the lack of attention afforded the relational side of the sexual union.

Implications of a Theology of Sex

There arise certain implications out of the preceding interpretations of the nature and purpose of sexuality. The first of these is the impossibility of establishing a wholesome and valid sexual relation without *agape* as the ruling element. Sexual union on any other plan than *agape* reduces the participating persons to things, and sexuality becomes separated from the person. The New Testament view of sexual relationships as a giving of one's body to the other individual, which involves the totality of the person, carries a great risk. Also, since the innermost being of the person is communicated, this knowledge can be properly given only in the context of man's highest kind of love. Therefore, only one who himself has experienced *agape* is able to bestow the gift of love in sexual union. This cannot be so except as those involved have surrendered their lives to God and received from him the *agape* out of which they act in this relationship.

That fidelity is demanded by the *agape* expected in sexual life is the second implication of this discussion. The one-flesh union which is established in sex union is caricatured unless there is an accompanying fidelity which guarantees that the risk or commitment of the union will not be betrayed. Fidelity here becomes the demonstration of *agape*. Fidelity is also demanded in the social implications of the sex act. These social implications must be fully accepted with the decision to commit one's person to another sexually, and they involve more than the mere possibility of pregnancy. These two, love and fidelity, are the highest virtues of sexual union.

From these comes a third implication on a practical plane. While unstated, it has been assumed that this sexual union which has been discussed finds its proper expression only in married love. This is part of the social implication of the act. The decision to accept another sexually in premarital or extramarital relation, regardless of circumstance, flouts the virtues of love and fidelity by accepting the person partially. Because the radical nature of sexuality reaches the inner depths of personal being, the participants need to be in position that the love which they express in union be both lasting and responsible.

The responsibility in sexual union comes from two directions. The first lies in the fact that when a person accepts another in sexual union, he becomes responsible for that person in sexuality and in *all* of the development of personality. In other words, the *whole* person must be accepted in both inner development and social setting. The second approach of responsibility lies in the very fact of potential procreation, whether it becomes a reality or not. It is not responsible love for two people to enter sexual union without their being in position to face the social obligations of a fruitful union should pregnancy occur. A one-flesh union is not valid until the two people who enter the relationship are ready to be completely responsible for each other.

The one flesh established symbolically in sexual union has further implications with regard to divorce. Jesus intended that once a one-flesh relationship had been established it was to be permanent, allowing no separation. It was not the intention of God that there should be a repudiation of life's deepest union. Where *agape* exists and a proper one-flesh union is established, there is no need for divorce or arrangement of termination.

It is in the absence of *agape*, or in Jesus' phrase "the hardness of men's hearts," that any arrangement for the repudiation of a union was ever made. Thus in the Christian ideal for marriage

and its establishment by one flesh, no place is given to the consideration of divorce. Where conditions are less than ideal and
unions are not established and maintained in *agape* (love), it will
be necessary to consider the propriety of divorce. In a later chapter we shall consider some of the "less than ideal" functions of
human sexuality and perhaps in this way see more of its true
purposes.

3. One Flesh—the Design for Marriage

At the heart of understanding the nature of Christian marriage is an understanding of Jesus' relational approach to life. He established a difficult but comprehensive goal in his reassertion that marriage is a one-flesh relationship. The apostle Paul, who interpreted Christ to the first missionary churches, exalted a parallel ideal. To him, the Christ-church relationship was the pattern for Christian marriage. These high goals form the ideals for the monogamous nature of marriage. Yet, they do not abrogate the fact that marriage is strictly a relationship of earthly life. In this chapter we will consider the biblical goal and the nature of the New Testament concept of marriage.

Marriage as "One Flesh"

Jesus stated the divine intention for marriage in the quotation: "But from the beginning of creation, 'God made them male and female.' For this reason a man shall leave his father and mother and be joined to his wife, and the two shall become one. So they are no longer two but one" (Mark 10:6-8). Uniting, then, the words of Genesis he makes "for this reason" (2:24) refer to the quotation, "So God created man in his own image, in the image of God he created him; male and female he created them" (1:27). This presents the male and female creation as the basis for exclusive attraction and the establishment of one flesh. The use of the future, i.e., "shall be" or "shall become," can be understood as a goal to be achieved in the uniting of two personal existences in marriage.

23

To comprehend the nature of this unity it is helpful to examine other such unities of relationship in the New Testament. For example, in Acts 4:32, "one . . . soul" describes the spiritual and emotional agreement of believers, while Paul's plea for the church to stand in "one spirit" (Phil. 1:27) is a desire for a unity of purpose and work. Moreover, Paul points to a unity of spirit between the individual and Christ, making the unity established between man and woman comparable to it. By this standard, then, the one-flesh relationship should include a fusion of "spirits" as well as bodies.

The relationship between believers comprising a church is usually expressed in terms of "one body" to describe the goal of unity of function (cf. Rom. 12:4 ff.; 1 Cor. 12:12). Unities of personal relationships referred to in the New Testament are expressed by various terms like "heart" (unity of emotions), "mind" (unity of purpose), "spirit" (unity of attitude and direction), and "body" (unity of function) to describe by synecdoche the unities of personalities.

The unity of one flesh does differ from the other unities described in the above paragraph in that there is a physical basis which becomes the symbol of the total union. Yet it must be emphasized that to become one flesh is not simply a physical union. The fact that one flesh is more than a physical union stems from two considerations. First, the term "flesh" or *sarx* in New Testament language does not mean, as has already been shown, simply physical material out of which the body is composed. *Sarx* is many times synonymously used with *psuche* (soul) and *pneuma* (spirit) to denote the whole of man's personality. The second is based upon the first in that the Hebrew view of personality may be described as holistic. Thus, what the flesh does is an action, expression, and commitment of the whole personality. The basic physical relationship of the one-flesh union gives expression to the unity of emotions, mind, purpose, attitudes, and functions.

Although, in a sense, a one-flesh union is established in every coming together of man and woman through sexual intercourse, not every such union is validated as one flesh in the New Testament understanding of personality and marriage. To become one flesh always remains a goal to be achieved in marriage, in the sexual relationship as well as in the totality of the personality. The realization of this goal depends, to a large extent, on the ability of man and woman entering marriage to incarnate the ideal which Paul presents in the Ephesian epistle. Here we consider Paul's understanding of the one-flesh relationship as presented in Ephesians.

The Head-Body Unity of Christ and the Church

Paul used the figure of Christ's unity with the church as the archetype for human marriage and exalted it as the goal toward which Christian marriage should move for an ideal relationship. The two subjects are completely intertwined in the passage, and it is necessary to follow the thought of the passage in detail for an understanding of the marriage relationship pictured. Which of the subjects takes precedence in the passage has been a matter of controversy, but here the emphasis upon human marriage will be considered. Here are the words of the text:

Wives, be subject to your husbands, as to the Lord. For the husband is the head of the wife as Christ is the head of the church, his body, and is himself its Savior. As the church is subject to Christ, so let wives also be subject in everything to their husbands. Husbands, love your wives, as Christ loved the church and gave himself up for her, that he might sanctify her, having cleansed her by the washing of water with the word, that the church might be presented before him in splendor, without spot or wrinkle or any such thing, that she might be holy and without blemish. Even so husbands should love their wives as their own bodies. He who loves his wife loves himself. For no man ever hates his own flesh, but nourishes and cherishes it, as Christ does the church, because we are members of his body. "For this reason a man shall leave his father and mother and be joined to his wife, and the two shall become one." This is a great mystery, and I take it to mean Christ and the church; however, let each one of you love his wife as himself, and let the wife see that she respects her husband (Eph. 5:22–33, RSV).

The opening admonition for the wife to be subject to the husband is in terms of the individual's surrender to God in the words "as to the Lord." It is assumed here that both partners are Christians and there is no incongruity between true love and subjection. The reason stated in the causal clause (v. 23) for the subjection is determined by the relative position which each occupies in the marriage relationship. It cannot be denied that the position given to the man as *head* of the wife is in keeping with the Judaism of that day.

This type of male authority in marriage as the standard Hebrew practice was known as *ba'al* marriage. Pedersen explains it by saying, *"Ba'al* always presupposes a psychic community, a whole, and a *ba'al* designates the ruling within this." [1] When viewed comparatively, male ascendancy is clearly demonstrated in the Hebrew culture. However, the context of the comparison and the qualification which Paul expresses in the analogy puts the relationship on a higher and therefore unoppressive plane.

The headship of the husband is analogous to the headship of Christ in the church; but Christ is the head of the Church because he is the Saviour of the body. It is therefore implied that the headship of the husband in some real sense makes him the preserver and sacrificing servant of the wife. At the same time, this consideration of the relative positions of the individual partners should not obscure the vital unity of the head-body analogy which is the major concern of the passage. Understanding thus the nature of the wife's subjecting to the husband, we see the completeness of the subjection asserted in verse 24. It is a voluntary subjection, however, as seen by the original force of "subject yourselves." Is it not true that, ideally, the will of the wife is perfectly at one with that of the husband? Yet, of course, there is a difference between Christ and the husband; there are no perfect husbands.

Love for the Body

Although the primary attention has been given to the husband as head in the opening verses, the section was addressed to the wives. Beginning with verse 25, the apostle addresses the husbands and calls attention to the manner and object of their love. The character of Christ's love for the church is made the measure of love in marriage. Christ's love here, as in Galatians 2:20, is attached to his surrender "on behalf of." The ideal love exalted is in every sense a self-giving, sacrificing love.

It is distinctly *agape*, both as contrasted with and related to other kinds of love, with which we are here concerned. Jesus posited *agape* as the foundation of all man's relationships in the Great Commandment: "You shall love the Lord your God with all your heart, and with all your soul, and with all your mind, and with all your strength" (Mark 12:30). Man's entire being is to be caught up in *agape* in his relationship to God. Likewise, this same *agape* is to characterize his relationship with other human beings.

To Paul, next to the believers 'in Christ' position, the most basic concept of the believer's life was his experience of the *agape* of God. This *agape* is divinely demonstrated and imparted in the full and free sacrifice of God's Son on behalf of sinful men (cf. Rom. 5:8; Gal. 2:20). Further, the omnipresent agency of God's love to the believer is the Holy Spirit (cf. Rom. 5:5). When this love becomes a grace of the believer's life, it has certain sterling qualities which identify it as a distinctively Christian attribute (cf. 1 Cor. 13), and it thus becomes the basis for all Christian work, "For the love of Christ controls us" (2 Cor. 5:14).

Here, then, is the illumination of whatever authority may be granted to the husband—because it rests on love and sacrifice. Chrysostom elaborated thus on the thought:

Wouldst thou have thy wife obedient unto thee, as the Church is to Christ? Take then thyself the same provident care for her, as Christ takes for the Church. Yea, even if it shall be needful for thee to give

thy life for her, . . . refuse it not. Though thou shouldst undergo all
this, yet wilt thou not, no, not even then, have done anything like
Christ. For thou indeed art doing it for one to whom thou art already
knit; but He for one who turned her back on Him and hated Him. In
the same way then as He laid at His feet her who turned her back on
Him, who hated, and spurned, and disdained Him; not by menaces,
nor by violence, nor by terror, nor by anything else of the kind, but by
his unwearied affection; so also do thou behave thyself toward thy wife.
. . . But the partner of one's life, the mother of one's children, the
foundation of everyone's joy, one ought never to chain down by fear
and menaces, but with love and good temper.[2]

The action of Christ, beginning in verse 26, is somewhat analogous to first-century marriage customs, with his deliverance
corresponding to the dowry, the "cleansing" to the bridal path,
and the act of presentation of the bride to Christ's presentation
of his church. The reference to cleansing is not necessarily a
reference to baptism, because here it is limited by "with the word."
The church as an eschatological bride must not only be thoroughly
cleansed but must be perfect in appearance and character. The
moral and spiritual purity expected by Christ of the church may
be projected as the ideal for a bride in human marriage.

The writer concerns himself again directly with the relationship
of husbands and wives with verse 28. The two concepts ascertained
before, namely that the husband occupies a "head" position in
the unity and that the manner of love is self-giving and sacrificing,
are the bases for husbands "to love their wives as their bodies."
Francis Beare (The Interpreter's Bible) correctly explains that
this last phrase, "their own bodies," does not refer to another being which is external to the husband but rather that the wives are
the "bodies" of the husbands. His interpretation continues,

The thought that the wife is the husband's "body" is correlative to
the thought that the husband is the "head" of the wife, and is parallel
with the thought that the church is Christ's body. Husband and wife
together are complementary parts of one personality; therefore it can
be said that "he who loves his wife loves himself." [3]

The only aspect of self-love in the husband's affection is that the wife is part of him or rather that each is a part of the unity and therefore part of each other. The husband is not to love his wife as he does his own physical body or to love the wife as being *his* body. He loves her because, to him as the head, she is *the* body.

The sense of verse 29 is: "It is not natural for a person to hate that which has become a part of him, but he nourishes it and gives it care, just as Christ does the church." In this sense conjugal love, like self-love, is natural. The nourishment and care, of which those who are members of his "body" have experience, is the practical expression of the ideal sacrificing love of the Christ-bridegroom.

The marriage union is the highest human demonstration of the ability of mutual love to bring unity and completeness to two otherwise incomplete beings. Love (*agape*), therefore, is presented as the ideal basis for sexual intercourse and the resulting one-flesh union, even though *eros* and *epithumia* are concommitant features of the physical aspect of sex.

To climax his argument for the corporeal unity described in the head-body relationship, Paul quotes the "one-flesh" statement from Genesis (v. 31). Back in verse 29, he substitutes the word "flesh" where he has been using "body" in anticipation of this quotation. The course of the discussion turns out that he has used the head-body relationship of Christ and the church to illuminate the meaning of "one flesh." In the next verse (32) the revelation of the one-flesh union is called a "mystery" (*musterion*). He says, "The mystery is great," notwithstanding translators who have changed and obscured the phrase. The word was translated in the Vulgate as *sacramentum*, from which the Roman Catholic doctrine of marriage as a sacrament was developed. The King James Version renders the phrase "this is a great mystery," which makes the predicate adjective an adjective.

"Mystery" in the New Testament refers to some new revelation which is made apparent in the gospel. The nature of human

marriage as the union in "one flesh" is revealed in the union of
Christ and the church. Here, "mystery" is a revelation known only
to those who understand and have experienced the Christ-church
relationship in its uniqueness. There are many such "mysteries"
which formerly were not known, but in the gospel become known.
This mystery is great because a great truth is revealed in the
Christ-church relationship.

The last verse of the section recapitulates the admonitions
given to the husband and wife in view of the preceding explanation for marriage as the head-body union. The admonition to the
wives to "fear" must be seen in relation to the preceding figure.
In this context the basic element in "fear" is reverence, by virtue
of the relationship entered, rather than dread of a ruling tyrant.
Love (*agape*) and fear (*phobos*) are here placed in a context of
near equivalence, separated chiefly by the relative positions of
man and woman in marriage. In view of other first-century customs, the positions of both husband and wife are greatly exalted.

The Hebrew husband stood in a far superior position to his
wife. His absolute authority began with his possession of the wife
as a sexual being but extended to his being able to divorce the
wife at will. The fundamental principle of the patriarchal family
was that the oldest male descendant was to be the absolute
authority as lawgiver, judge, and ruler over his family.

Out of the foregoing examination of Paul's Christ-church
description emerges the ideal for marriage as a head-body unity,
which is a goal to be achieved. The man is the "head" of the
unity, not simply because he is male but because he assumes
the husband role in the relationship. The woman is the "body" of
the unity, not by virtue of her sex alone but because she accepts the
wife's role. Ideally, the husband's role is to love the wife sacri-
fically with a primary concern for the welfare of the body (his
wife). This is love (*agape*) exercising itself in marriage.

To determine the existence and place of *agape* in marriage it is
necessary to consider its relation to other kinds of love—*eros* and

epithumia. Nygren [4] makes a wide cleavage between *agape* and *eros* by identifying the latter as the desire of the soul of man to attain salvation by seeking detachment from earthly objects of desire and by seeking after heavenly things. While this concept of platonic *eros* is not found in the New Testament, it is present in human experience as the anthropocentric kind of love. On the other hand, *epithumia* (desire) is found in the New Testament and is presented in such a way that it may be termed the driving power of man's *eros* relationships. It can allow a being to relate himself as an "I" to a "thou." *Eros* and *epithumia* have had their rightful places in biblical marriage when they have led to and become superseded by *agape.*

Ideally, the woman in the role of the wife "subjects" herself to her husband in the safe atmosphere of love and reverences him in his role. This subjection and reverence are only possible, of course, if the wife exercises love also. Thus the head-body ideal of Paul gives practical definition to the roles of husbands and wives in the one-flesh relationship. Further, the head-body figure emphasizes the interdependent nature of marriage. It is implied in this entire discussion that marriage is relational in character and the ideals of a head-body relationship would be possible only for those who had submitted themselves first to God.

The first foundation of marriage, then, is the concept of love (*agape*) as found in the New Testament. It is a theocentric love but must become the experience of believers. In the marriage union it has opportunity for its highest expression and work, when aided by other kinds of love and kept constant by fidelity. This love is neither easily understood nor readily experienced. Its comprehension is based primarily on the believer's experience in Christ and demands a mature Christian faith for its realization. Yet, it is basic to Christian marriage.

These goals are Christian concepts of marriage. Viewing marriage as having such profound significance, we now turn to look at the monogamous nature of Christian marriage.

Should Marriage Be Monogamous?

The merits of monogamy or polygamy obviously are not discussed in the New Testament as such. The biblical argument for monogamy begins with the creation accounts of human bisexual life. The fact that one woman was created for one man and that *adham* (man) was created as male and female militates for monogamous marriage. Emil Brunner (*The Divine Imperative*) has developed the argument for monogamy on what he designates as the "divine order of creation." The will of God is to be discovered in the "giveness" of the order, and in marriage this concerns two facts. The first is that a child as a subject is uniquely related and dependent on two other subjects for his existence. This involves a unique and unparalleled relation of three persons whose human existences are bound up together. Added to the trinity of being is the given fact of human sexual love which is monistic and, when genuine, exclusive of others in this same relation. In view of these given facts, says Brunner, the order of creation calls for monogamy, and Jesus, he claims, used this argument.

However, if monogamy was the intention in creation it was certainly not followed in the history of Israel. The patriarchs, judges, and kings of Israel practiced polygamy profusely. The practice of using handmaidens of the wife to beget children was not considered polygamous. The Deuteronomic legislation forbade polygamy to the king but made provisions for the children of bigamists as though it was expected (cf. Deut. 21:15–17). Polygamy was reported in most ancient societies by such men as Herodotus and Plutarch.

There is, however, in addition to the record of numerous instances of polygamy, the clear record in the Old Testament of the unsuitability of this arrangement. Inevitably, jealousy and strife arose in marriage. Stronger than legislation against polygamy, the Old Testament teaches its evils by example. On the other hand, the marriages, wives, and husbands that were exalted as ideal were monogamous.

The idyllic picture of a wife in Proverbs (chap. 31) presupposes monogamy. When the prophets discuss marriage or use it as a figure of divine-human relations, monogamy is assumed. The creation account, as well as the words of the marriage institution, gives marriage a monogamous nature: "Therefore a man leaves his father and his mother and cleaves to his wife, and they become one flesh" (Gen. 2:24). Several pieces of Old Testament legislation presupposed monogamy as the rule (cf. Ex. 21:9; Lev. 18:18; and Deut. 21:15–17). The Mishnah and Talmud continue to exalt this monogamous ideal.

Legislation against adultery was based more on property rights of the husband than on ethical grounds. Therefore, the term "adultery" was generally applied to women as there could scarcely be such a thing as infidelity on the man's part in such a culture. The fear of adultery was due to the fact that if a man's possession (his wife or his daughter) was taken by another man, it would not then be possible to determine the father of the child from such a union.

While Jesus did not expressly discuss the monogamous constitution of marriage, his brief references assumed it. The one-flesh union to which he pointed could exist only in a monogamous marriage and his discussion of divorce and adultery would have little point if multiple marriages were expected.

Likewise, Paul's discussion of marriage and its problems assumes a monogamous union. It is demanded for the realization of the "head-body" ideal. The character of love described in that relationship would be impossible in a polygamous system. In specific directions Paul gives no consideration to any other than marriages of one man and one woman. In fact, the situations to which he addresses himself reflect, in general, monogamy as a standard. Paul at least states that according to the Law it is adultery for a woman to marry another man (cf. Rom. 7:1–3); howbeit, the Jews had a double standard for the freedom of the sexes.

The qualifications for various church offices described in the Pastorals include the phrases "husband of one wife" (1 Tim. 3:2, 12; Titus 1:6) and "wife of one man" (1 Tim. 5:9). There are three possible interpretations of this phrase—a married person, i.e., not single; not divorced and remarried; not a polygamist. Of the three, the last is most in keeping with the environment of the early church, although the second might be included. With this standard for bishops, deacons, and widows it is evident that monogamy was considered a necessity for Christian marriage.

It appears conclusive that both Jesus and his interpreters assumed monogamy alone as the intention of God for man in marriage. This is not the only question whose answer must be arrived at by implication and example, but our next consideration does have more direct evidence.

Earthly or Eternal?

Another question which poses itself with regard to marriage is the duration of the union. Is it an earthly or an eternal relationship? Jesus spoke directly to the question and in Paul's "in Christ" theology there are some conclusive answers for this question. A section in Mark which deals with this problem is called an apothegm, meaning that the narrative and description center in a culminating saying of Jesus.

Sadducees came to him, who say that there is no resurrection; and they asked him a question, saying, "Teacher, Moses wrote for us that if a man's brother dies and leaves a wife, but leaves no child, the man must take the wife, and raise up children for his brother. There were seven brothers; the first took a wife, and when he died left no children; and the second took her, and died, leaving no children; and the third likewise; and the seven left no children. Last of all the woman also died. In the resurrection whose wife will she be? For the seven had her as wife." Jesus said to them, "Is not this why you are wrong, that you know neither the scriptures nor the power of God? For when they rise from the dead, they neither marry nor are given in marriage, but are like angels in heaven. And as for the dead being raised, have you not read in the book of Moses, in the passage about the bush, how God said to him, 'I am the God of Abraham, and the God of Isaac, and the God of Jacob'? He is not God of the dead, but of the living; you are quite wrong (Mark 12:18–27, RSV).

This levirate example was used merely to introduce the questions about the resurrection and was a stock *reductio ad absurdum* to deny the resurrection and eternal life by the Sadducees. It is a typical rabbinic debate. The interest for the constitution of marriage lies in the answer of Jesus. His reference to their lack of knowledge of the Scriptures may refer to 1 Enoch which says, "You are ever living spirits, . . . therefore I have not created wives for you." (See also Tobit 12:9.) Angels were thus looked upon as sexless creatures for whom marriage was impossible and unnecessary. The resurrection life of men, he was implying, will be of the same nature. E. P. Gould observes, "He has power not only to raise but so to change the body that marriage ceases to be one of its functions." [5]

The marriage relationship, like many other relationships of life, is adapted to an earthly existence, but this does not abrogate the divine origin. Cole summarizes the passage in a satisfactory explanation by saying:

> The emphasis in Jesus' answer is based upon the fact that at the end of history, the exclusive relationships of this world are banished. All will love one another equally before God. He was not looking forward to release from the body and its degrading passions, regarding sex and marriage as evil. He expected the resurrection of the flesh in the tradition of Hebrew naturalism.[6]

Hence, marriage is an earthly relationship, and the implications of this will be considered later with regard to remarriage.

Paul used a relevant analogy in which he stated a principle for this question in Galatians 3:23–29.

> Now before faith came, we were confined under the law, kept under restraint until faith should be revealed. So that the law was our custodian until Christ came, that we might be justified by faith. But

now that faith has come, we are no longer under a custodian; for in
Christ Jesus you are all sons of God, through faith. For as many of
you as were baptized into Christ have put on Christ. There is neither
Jew nor Greek, there is neither slave nor free, there is neither male nor
female; for you are all one in Christ Jesus. And if you are Christ's,
then you are Abraham's offspring, heirs according to promise (RSV).

At the beginning of the passage the apostle is continuing a
discussion of a believer's relationship with Christ as opposed to
a relationship with the Law. He describes this relationship as a
faith relationship which makes men "sons of God." This
reminds him of the universality of the relationship through faith
and he comes in verse 28 to enunciate the principle of no distinctions. This principle describes the equality of positions believers
occupy "in Christ." Certainly human, earthly differences that may
exist between classes mentioned are not necessarily affected by
the principle. He is simply stating that these differences do not
obtain in the spiritual realm.

The principle is implied and referred to several times in Paul's
writings. In discussing the new nature of the redeemed individual,
Paul tells the Colossians that it has nothing to do with earthly
differences (cf. 3:10–11). Again, the unity of the body is called
for on the basis of equality existing between members, regardless
of their earthly positions (cf. 1 Cor. 12:13). Distinctions have
been abolished as having any influence in the access to God
through Christ (cf. Eph. 2:13–18).

If, on the basis of this principle, earthly distinctions have no
bearing on the individual's access to God through Christ or
position "in Christ," then life beyond that which is earthly does
not retain these distinctions. In other words, Paul's concept of
spiritual life would not recognize the marriage relationship as anything but an earthly arrangement; in fact, he states that death
dissolves the marriage bond (cf. Rom. 7:2).

In this chapter we have envisioned the breadth of the marriage
relationship in the "one-flesh" concept as well as reviewing some
of the limiting questions about marriage. The value of such study

is contained in the fact that in the Christian view it is important not only to know what human life is but also what it ought to become. The fact that the "one-flesh" concept is a goal should not color it as unrealistic. The continuous striving of the church to come into an ideal relationship with her head should be paralleled by a reaching toward a realization of "ideal marriage" by committed Christian partners. Unless these come to some clear view of the true nature of marriage, their strivings will be in vain.

The question of monogamy may appear to have little significance for our present Western culture, but two considerations make the question more relevant. First, simultaneous polygamy is not far removed from "successive polygamy" which has invaded Western culture through endless rounds of divorce and remarriage. In fact, divorce is often little more than legal circumvention of the prohibition of polygamy. Secondly, the amalgamation of cultures, which is accelerating constantly, means that many Christians will confront or be living in cultures which are not monogamous. The question will inevitably be raised before Christians, if not within them.

At the same time, the earthly nature of the marriage relationship just discussed will likely be more recognized due to the generally lighter view of marriage of present cultures. This question has greatest relevance for those widows or widowers who contemplate remarriage. A thorough understanding of the theological view of marriage would alleviate the conflict of loyalties which some experience in this question. However, it must be emphasized that the term "earthly," as here applied to marriage, does not equate with "of no importance" or "secular." Marriage remains a sacred relationship for human existence.

4. The Purposes of Marriage

Just as there are goals in marriage to create the ideal relationship discussed in the previous chapter, there are purposes and functions in marriage which bring divine benefits to both individuals and society. Not all of these purposes and functions are explicit in either of the Testaments. Some of these are simply assumed in the New Testament on the basis of Old Testament creation accounts and of its ethical enactments. Still others are more or less emphasized in the New Testament because of its ethic which has a decided relational character. In this chapter we are concerned to discover these for Christian marriage.

In Roman Catholic theology Thomas Aquinas took the blessings of marriage stated by Augustine and equated them with ends of marriage, dividing them into primary and secondary categories.[1] D. S. Bailey rejects this division and suggests that marriage has different ends or purposes rather than primary and secondary ends.[2] Both of these approaches, however, are dangerous if they leave the impression that marriage is simply a means to an end.

The ideally unitive relationship of marriage is intended as an end in itself, even though there are functions which are served when these ideals are realized. A treatment more in keeping with the nature of Christian marriage is to list these ends under the heading of creative and preventive purposes and functions.

Creative Purposes

Fellowship.—Among the creative functions of marriage, none is more basic than fellowship. This is the mutual exchange of

38

human experiences by persons who open their lives to one another. The idea of fellowship is embedded in the creation account of man and woman in the words, "It is not good that man should be alone" (Gen. 2:18). It is also inherent in the very nature of the "one-flesh" and "head-body" relationship. These concepts imply the closest proximity in human relationships. Marriage offers the opportunity for communication of person with person and holds the secret of creative interactivity.

Wholesome communication is one of the most redemptive functions of human life, especially through marriage. Personality is encouraged to completeness through the communication of marriage. Even though he rejects the primary and secondary categories, Bailey agrees that the unitive end is primary in marriage.

Human sexuality also suggests a fellowship purpose in marriage, as noted by Otto Piper when he says, "The fact that man receives a female companion, and not another male, shows that sex character and the sex desires are regarded as significant and valuable primarily from the standpoint of fellowship."[3] This certainly is one of the most intimate and potentially meaningful of human experiences to be mutually shared in marriage. Brunner feels that marriage is an ontological necessity, stating that "our whole existence is framed on the assumption that our fundamental reality consists in the relation between *two* persons and that *no* human being can ever attain fullness of being as an isolated individual but only through surrender to another person." [4]

Other admonitions in the New Testament show that fellowship is expected as a function of marriage. Paul admonishes, "Do not be mismated with unbelievers" (2 Cor. 6:14). He bases this advice, in the rest of the verse, on the fact that there can be no partnership or fellowship in such a union. Considerateness of husbands is encouraged by Peter because man and wife are joint partakers of grace (cf. 1 Peter 3:7).

The fellowship of marriage can become a symbol of divine-human fellowship if the marriage union is endowed with the graces of the divine-human union. As the fellowship of marriage is experienced between two persons they are better able to experience and understand the fellowship which ought to exist between each of them and God. The purposes of fellowship in marriage are major concerns to Christian partners. If fellowship is not present there will be little opportunity for establishing a vital relationship. It is the opportunity for fellowship in human marriage which prevents the next purpose considered from being a merely biological function.

Procreation.—Historically, the procreative function of marriage has received major attention and is the primary purpose of marriage in the sacramental view. Roman Catholic theologians have long claimed this as the sole primary function. According to E. C. Messenger, the increase of the church is the basis for the emphasis on this function.[5] The dictum "be fruitful and multiply" (Gen. 1:22) is made the biblical basis for this exclusive emphasis. In reality, this one-sided emphasis is a reflection of the influence of Greek philosophical thought upon early Roman Catholic theology. The church accepted the Greek idea that physical functions are inherently evil and found justification for marriage only in the population of the church.[6]

The fact that in the nature of marriage a one-flesh relationship is symbolically established by sexual union does give the procreative function a basic place in marriage. Thus, Bailey can say "that its chief institutional (and biological) purpose is procreation."[7] Yet, because a marriage should ideally be fruitful is not to say that every marriage must be unrestrictedly procreative. The other purposes and functions of marriage cannot be ignored and marriage itself be made subservient to this one purpose.

The question of procreation is given almost no attention in the New Testament. Yet, it is assumed in the New Testament, as would be expected from the Jewish milieu out of which the New Testament was written. Two references (1 Tim. 2:15; 5:14) give childbearing as one of the many duties of women, but the reference to marriage is quite indirect. On the other hand, the eschatological shadow which falls over most of the New Testament reflects something of an abhorrence of childbirth, as well as of many of the other normal duties of earthly living (cf. Matt. 24:19; 1 Cor. 7:27).

Thus, while it is tacitly assumed in the New Testament that procreation is a major purpose in marriage, procreation does not receive the emphasis placed upon it in the Old Testament or in Christian theology. The other purposes and functions are asserted as much as this one. In fact, it would be incongruous with the relational character of Jesus' ethic to emphasize this function to the neglect or disparagement of other functions in marriage. There is nothing to prevent procreation from being complementary to the other purposes in the marriage union.

Both of the two creative functions of marriage just discussed can make valuable contributions to the other creative function of edification in marriage.

Edification.—Reference has been made earlier to the potential of sexuality to serve in the sanctification of the person. In the same vein the marriage relationship itself also serves to enhance the spiritual life of the participants when its ideals are accepted. Where the partners are believers, the marriage relationship furnishes an opportunity for the experience of love (*agape*) unparalleled in any other relationship.

Married Christian love is the one place where the total personalities of the participants can be risked in a safe atmosphere. In such a marriage the "fruits of the spirit" which Paul recognizes and recommends can be experienced. These are love, joy, peace, patience, kindness, goodness, faithfulness, gentleness, and self-control (cf. Gal. 5:22–23).

Peace, especially, is to characterize marriage, according to the ideal of Paul (cf. 1 Cor. 7:15). The practice of Christian virtues is also encouraged by Peter when he states that the ideal for wives is the presence of a "gentle and quiet spirit" (1 Peter 3:4). This gentleness is typical of Christ himself and was a standard admonition in the ethical code of early Christianity.

An atmosphere for prayer is emphasized as a necessity for the marriage relationship in the New Testament. Paul encouraged that proper provision for prayer be made (cf. 1 Cor. 7:5), while Peter pleaded for an atmosphere where "your prayers be not hindered" (1 Peter 3:7).

Some attention is given in the New Testament to the part the believer plays in the sanctification and salvation of an unbelieving partner. Paul assures his readers that an unbelieving father does not make the children illegitimate (cf. 1 Cor. 7:14). In such an instance of a divided marriage, Peter exhorts the wife to such conduct as will result in the salvation of a husband (cf. 1 Peter 3:1–7). It is important to note, however, that the apostle is willing to depend upon the influence of the wife in the demonstration of her Christian faith and not upon manipulation or coercive words.

Before Paul had enunciated the principles of calling, Jesus had assumed them when he referred to voluntary celibacy as applying to certain people who had received a gift for it (cf. Matt. 19:12). Paul makes the same application to unmarried life, seeing it as a "special gift from God." He then implies, when he uses the words "one of one kind and one of another" (1 Cor. 7:7), that if celibacy is a gift, so also is the married state. The only "other" state or gift for man besides celibacy would be marriage. In the New Testament a person's calling to a particular office or state is usually based upon his *charisma* or gift (cf. Rom. 12:3–8; 1 Cor. 12:4–11). Therefore, marriage or celibacy must be in accord with one's *charisma*.

The charismatic gift of celibacy is practical in terms of service for the kingdom of God rather than being meritorious in the sense of ascetic superiority. No special credit is attached to the gift except as one honors and serves Christ. A life of peace and service to the kingdom of God is more important than celibacy or marriage (cf. 1 Cor. 7:17–24). David Mace sees the true proportions of marriage as a calling when he states, "Marriage can be truly a vocation only when it is seen as part of a greater vocation still." [8] Christian calling, then, as a theological foundation for marriage, should determine one's decision as to whether to marry or not. This decision is based upon one's position in Christ and the nature of his service and vocation. Marriage, from a Christian point of view, is seen as one important aspect of every believer's total experience of a "calling" in Christ.

Marriage as a calling, then, has at least one forceful implication. The believer is as responsible to God for what he makes of his marriage, which is in accord with his *charisma*, as he is for occupational vocation. Or, to state it otherwise, marriage is to be viewed as an integral aspect of the Christian's total 'in Christ' calling.

In view of the fact that the New Testament was largely written for the encouragement of Christians in their spiritual life, it is not surprising that such emphasis is given to edification in marriage. This striving for spiritual edification in marriage becomes part of the total redemption of believers. Redemption, as conceived and applied in the New Testament, permeates and affects every relationship of man. The marriage relationship is enhanced when it serves such lofty purposes. Here again it is assumed that such marriage as is conceived in the New Testament is that of believers whose lives are committed to God.

These creative purposes, when recognized and realized, serve to fulfil the sanctity of the marriage relationship. In their realization, both individual and corporate evil is curbed. We also turn now to recognize that, in addition to the creative purposes just described, marriage offers certain benefits which can be best labeled as preventive functions. These functions are necessary for both individuals and society.

Preventive Functions

Control of passion.—Sexual passion is recognized in the New Testament as one of the most powerful forces of normal human life. Men have sought to deal with it in a variety of ways. The patristic writers urged as complete suppression of sexual desire as possible. Jesus insisted that man is expected to control his passion so that it does not become lust: "I say to you that every one who looks at a woman lustfully has already committed adultery with her in his heart" (Matt. 5:28, RSV).

Paul recognized that a life of celibacy is a gift quite different from the usual capacities of men when he used the phrase: "Whoever is firmly established in his heart, being under no necessity but having his desire under control" (1 Cor. 7:37, RSV). Paul thus gave control of passion as a reason for getting married. While admittedly this is not a very high motive for marriage, in his view, time was so short that only those who were compelled by strong desires should enter marriage. Most of the other biblical writers also recognized passion as a potent force to be controlled in human life. Various words, as will be seen in a later chapter, were used which had connotations of unbridled passion.

Passion does serve a useful function in life when it leads to the physical expression of married love. However, when it becomes the ruling appetite and exists outside the marriage relationship it becomes lust. Marriage serves the purpose of taking sexual desire and channeling it into love.

When marital adjustment has been achieved to some measure of completeness, passion is integrated into the marriage relationship. The mutual consideration of husbands and wives for each other's sexual needs directs these desires exclusively toward the marriage partners. Paul recognized this when he exhorted married couples to engage in conjugal relations, lest passion should become temptation (cf. 1 Cor. 7:1–6). In this very real problem for many individuals and much of society, then, marriage has the potential for this preventive function. The function of the control of passion is more apparent and personal than the next function suggested here. Yet, there is a vital connection between control of passion and the dissolution of society.

The dissolution of society.—Family is the basic unit of society in the biblical account of human creation. The Hebrews accepted this as standard for all their marriage institutions. Pedersen describes the concept of family (*mishpachah*) as being "the essential factor of community" and "the basis of all definitions, and that it immediately presents itself wherever the Israelite wants to define community." [9] Within the *mishpachah* the husband-father was the important person, but a fruitful wife was looked upon as an inherent necessity. Handmaidens used to beget children were looked upon as doing the duty of the wife for her.

This family unit idea was carried into the tribal and national government where each of these units was patterned simply as an amplification of a family unit. In fact, the individual's standing and security depended upon his family, and his actions were a reflection of honor or disgrace to the family as well as to himself.

As long as Israel remained a rural people the sons married and incorporated their families within the larger family unit of the tribe. All the family was responsible to the oldest male descendant who had the authority for civil government within the tribe. Through the vicissitudes of national life and the development of urban communities the tribal unit gradually broke down, but the family unit remained the basic arrangement of Hebrew society. Thus, biblical writers assumed the benefits to society through a wholesome family life.

Again, it is by implication that the New Testament treats of the dissolution of society. Neither Jesus nor his early followers were especially concerned with the preservation of culture and society; rather, they were concerned about preparation for the kingdom of God. However, as the early churches began to be established there arose need for ethical codes of Christian conduct in matters of family life, and the relationships of family life began to receive attention. Most of these codes were based on Hebrew concepts of family and Hebrew morals. Remnants of such codes appear in the New Testament epistles, such as Ephesians, Colossians, 1 Peter, and the Pastorals. Some of the common elements pointed out by Selwyn were the subjection of wives to husbands, modesty in dress by women, and love of wives by husbands.[10]

The legitimacy of children born to a union of believer and unbeliever, Paul explains, is based on the assumption that proper marriage is prerequisite to honorable society. Thus, he says, "the unbelieving husband is consecrated through his wife, and the unbelieving wife is consecrated through her husband. Otherwise, your children would be unclean, but as it is they are holy" (1 Cor. 7:14, RSV).

There are various admonitions placed in the context of marriage relationships which assume that Christian marriage gives validity to the family as a unity of society. (See Col. 3:18 ff. and 1 Peter 3:1–7.) The marriage relationship appears in the list of "human institutions" to which Christians are to give themselves in subjection. "Be subject for the Lord's sake to every human institution" (1 Peter 2:13). The admonitions given are directed toward the establishment of a union in which the foundations of society can be experienced by husbands, wives, and children.

Present society in the United States is being thrust for its stability upon the resources of the family. The impersonalization of social life and the development of complex urban life have pushed the members of the family more into dependence on one another. Yet, as Gibson Winter points out, the indefiniteness of family authority and the changing family patterns have given rise to instability in present society.[11] The validity of the Hebrews' assumption of the importance of the family as a basic unit of society is nowhere more clearly illustrated than in the present vicissitudes of American culture.

The marriage union uniquely offers this opportunity for the prevention of society's dissolution, as marriage is conceived in the Christian view of home life. In Christian marriage the atmosphere is conducive to the learning of values which society has to offer. Again, because of the position of subjection of life to which the Christian offers himself there may develop within the family a wholesome respect for society's valid institutions. Not only may the dissolution of society be prevented but there is that within the Christian ethic which is redemptive for society.

For society, Christian marriages are "the salt of the earth." The demonstration of Christian qualities between husbands and wives can do much to establish these practices and attitudes in other relationships of society. The influence of the secret and intimate relationships of husbands and wives are never confined to their own lives, but constantly the waves of harmonious or troubled lives are felt in the larger sea of society.

The purposes and functions discussed here furnish a valid test for Christian marriage. To the degree that a marriage serves these purposes and functions it is becoming a "one-flesh" Christian relationship. While these purposes and functions should be reached for in marriage, they should appear also as the natural result of a unitive relationship. Like the experience of happiness in marriage, these results should appear without constant effort to attain them. In the same sense that all great art is seemingly effortless, Christian marriage should achieve these standards. If these purposes and functions are realized, further benefits and blessings can also be expected from the union of two committed believers.

5. Sexual Aberrations

The realism of the Bible presents the other side of sexuality as well as its true purposes. When sin enters human life it often enters life completely, and nowhere is it more poignantly demonstrated than in sexuality. Like marriage itself, sexuality is a fragile relationship in its truest purposes and lends itself easily to perversions of all kinds in human life. Jesus and New Testament writers saw these perversions as expressions of the perverseness of men's hearts and sought their correction as a means of redemption of human life.

More is said directly, in fact, about the perversions of sexuality in the New Testament than about its true dimensions. Discussions of these distortions, however, have the value of placing in focus the intention of God for human sexuality. Paganism, confronted by the gospel, certainly presented different standards of sexual morality than were implicit in the gospel. It was difficult then, as now, to denounce perversions of sexuality without seeming to decry sexuality itself. In this chapter we shall attempt to understand further the nature and purposes of sexuality by recognizing its misappropriations and the prohibitions against them.

Porneia (Fornication)

The basic connotation of *porneia* is that of prostitution. People, both men and women, who were prostitutes were identified by the words *pornoi* and *pornai* (cf. Matt. 21:32; 1 Cor. 5:9–11; 6:9; Eph. 5:5; 1 Tim. 1:10; Heb. 13:4). Sex is viewed in this practice as a merchandisable item; i.e., it is something which can be detached from the rest of the person and purchased for use. Paul expresses the charge against this by saying, "The body is not meant for immorality, but for the Lord" (1 Cor. 6:13).

In part, the revolt against *porneia* in the New Testament may be a rebellion against a background of sacred prostitution. Such is the description of prostitution in Revelation 17:4–5:

> The woman was arrayed in purple and scarlet, and bedecked with gold and jewels and pearls, holding in her hand a golden cup full of abominations and the impurities of her fornication; and on her forehead was written a name of mystery: "Babylon the great, mother of harlots and of earth's abominations."

Many surrounding religions had a history of sacred prostitution in which funds received were dedicated to the cause of religion. Whereas, in these religions prostitution was considered a sacred duty, in the New Testament it is associated with impurity and licentiousness (cf. 2 Cor. 12:21) in such a way as to suggest that the practice rendered a person morally and ceremonially unclean.

A birth resulting from *porneia* was considered illegitimate as assumed in the reply of the Pharisees: "We were not born of fornication, we have one Father, even God" (John 8:41, RSV). The figure here refers to spiritual parentage of course, but the implication is obvious. Prohibition against *porneia* was early placed upon Christians in the Jerusalem conference: "Write to them to abstain from the pollutions of idols and from unchastity and from what is strangled and from blood" (Acts 15:20). B. W. Bacon has suggested that a mystical belief was responsible for the decrees of prohibition against both foods for idols and sexual intercourse with pagans to avoid being united with alien life, including demons.[1]

Porneia is denounced on the ground that it runs contrary to the will of God for the body, i.e., sanctification of the whole person: "This is the will of God . . . that you abstain from immorality" (1 Thess. 4:3). *Porneia* is included in the list of vices which make up the fruit of the flesh (cf. Gal. 5:19) and, as such,

should be put to death or eradicated from the life of the Christian
(cf. Col. 3:5). To be sure, Jesus' concern over this practice was
not simply in the practice alone; he pointed to its source—a perverted heart or inner life (cf. Matt. 15:19).

Here again we are confronted with the New Testament concern
for the whole person in the fact that sexual perversion cannot
be separated from the perversion of the entire personality. The
very variety of forms of *porneia* is indicative of the revolt against
any kind of sexual perversion. Paul even used the word as the
general classification for adultery or incest (cf. 1 Cor. 5:1): "It
is actually reported that there is immorality among you . . . for
a man is living with his father's wife." He also suggests that the
antidote for *porneia* is marriage (cf. 1 Cor. 7:2).

The specific connotation of *porneia* as prostitution comes from
its Old Testament background. Although it is used in a figurative
sense, fornication in the Old Testament was to prostitute one's
self or Israel spiritually and religiously (cf. 2 Chron. 21:11; Isa.
23:17). It was viewed not so much as a single incident but more
as a way of life. The practice entailed especially the habit of
Israel's laying herself open to any and all religious influences.
Also, in the book of Revelation, this figurative sense is carried
over where the mythical Babylon is presented as the harlot who
has perverted peoples, nations, and kings (chaps. 17-18).

Two factors combine in view of the above discussion to establish the destructiveness of *porneia*. First is the attempt to separate
sexuality from the person and reduce it to a merchandisable item.
The second is the resulting irresponsible commitment of one's
self sexually to any or all, as though sexuality had no radical
meaning as a one-flesh relationship. The terms for sexual perversion often overlap in the New Testament, as evidenced in the
following discussion of adultery.

Adultery

A second sexual sin which the New Testament assails is that
of adultery. The word for adultery *moicheia* basically means un-

faithfulness to the marital commitment. The Old Testament commandment, "Thou shalt not commit adultery," is well respected in the New Testament. The New Testament word certainly has a Hebrew background. The Jewish Encyclopedia defines it thus:

Sexual intercourse of a married woman with any other man than her husband. The crime can be committed only by and with a married woman; for the unlawful intercourse of a married man with an unmarried woman is not technically adultery in Jewish law. When the adultery is committed with a married woman who is within the prohibited degrees of consanguinity or affinity, the crime becomes *incest* . . . for organized society was impossible unless it punished this crime which saps the very root of social life. "Thou shalt not commit adultery" is not merely a command not to tamper with the domestic affairs of another, but a warning to refrain from unsettling the foundations of society.[2]

Stunned by the tragedy of his own wife's infidelity, Hosea saw adultery as a reflection of Israel's infidelity to Jehovah. Against the concept of the covenant relationship of Israel and Jehovah, the course of the former earned the designation of "adulteress." With Israel as the prototype in action, idolatry and infidelity to God became the inference of adultery in spiritual life. Thus the adjective of *moicheia* is used to describe a generation of people as being especially faithless or unfaithful to God: "Whoever is ashamed of me and of my words in this adulterous and sinful generation" (Mark 8:38).

The morally rebellious are considered adulterers in the New Testament (cf. Luke 18:11; 1 Cor. 6:9). Special emphasis is given to adulterous desire and the fact that adultery is committed in (and proceeds from) the heart. Jesus especially emphasized this in his words, "I say to you that every one who looks at a woman lustfully has already committed adultery with her in his heart" (Matt. 5:28; cf. 15:19). Here again Jesus deals with the inner dynamics of the person rather than with a simple prohibition of actions.

The absolute ethic of Jesus would destroy and eradicate the

root of adultery. He extended the coverage of the term to include
more than those who sought extramarital sexual companionship.
Those guilty of adultery (and as such in need of God's redeeming
grace) include all in whom the desire for extramarital relations
has arisen. Hence, these must be included in later New Testament
lists of those who are unacceptable to God without an experience
of repentance and cleansing from these sins. In fact, as will be
seen later, Jesus broadened the term to include those who flouted
the ideal of God for marriage by divorce (cf. Mark 10:11–12).
Perhaps here, however, it is well to remind ourselves that Jesus
did not make this the (or an) unpardonable sin.

In summary then, the perversion of *moicheia* is that the person,
including his sexuality, has been committed to one person in
marriage but he is unfaithful to this prior commitment. There
is no specific consideration given in the New Testament to premarital sexual relations. However, in view of the breadth of Jesus'
understanding of personal commitment in marriage and his
definition of *moicheia*, there would be no room for irresponsible
promiscuity of sexuality outside marriage. This would hold true
regardless of the existing future plans of those involved. The
establishment of one flesh symbolically in sexual relationship finds
its proper place only when it expresses what is in fact a reality:
the unreserved commitment of two people to each other in marriage. Overlapping usages appear among all these terms of sexual
aberrations.

Uncleanness

Another sin which has sexual connotations attached to it is
what is called *akatharsia*. This word is used in the Septuagint
for "uncleanness," whether from pollution or disease, and has
chiefly ceremonial connotation. There is an instance in the New
Testament where physical impurity or uncleanness is referred to
(cf. Matt. 23:27), but the primary use is that the word refers to
sexual immorality.

Akatharsia in this sense is the result of another sin, *aselgeia* (uncontrolled morals, loose living), as Paul notes in Ephesians 4:19: "They have become callous and have given themselves up to licentiousness, greedy to practice every kind of uncleanness."

Among the sins considered uncleanness is homosexuality or "the dishonoring of their bodies among themselves" (Rom. 1: 24–26). It is classed with *aselgeia* as a sin for which there ought to be lasting repentance (cf. 2 Cor. 12:21).

Paul considered *akatharsia* a practice of pagan society as opposed to what is Christian, as he shows in Romans 6:19: "Just as you once yielded your members to impurity and to greater and greater iniquity, so now yield your members to righteousness for sanctification." He found it standing in opposition to sanctification and holiness to which the Christian is called (cf. 1 Thess. 4:7). Hence, it is a sin not so much of specific practice as it is an attitude of the person toward his sexual behavior. This state may be the result of any kind of sexual sin which renders the person unfit for sanctification and a properly oriented sex life.

Licentiousness

Like uncleanness, licentiousness (*aselgeia*) is more an orientation of life or kind of commitment than a particular practice, as expressed in Ephesians 4:19. The term is used to describe the inner character of a person and appears in the lists of general immoralities (see Mark 7:22; 1 Peter 4:3). In 2 Peter 2:2, 7–8 and Jude 4, *aselgeia* refers to general ungodliness and disobedience. However, Paul's use of it is usually placed in the context of sexual sins; e.g., it is classed with *akatharsia* and *porneia* (fornication) in 2 Corinthians 12:21 and Galatians 5:19. Also, it is coupled with "debauchery" in Romans 13:13, where it has the import of a sexual looseness upon which all of the attention of the person is concentrated.

This word (*aselgeia*) is the widest of the terms used for sexual immorality and often includes more than sexual sins. The word *aselgeia* began with the meaning "without being spellbound" or "not capable of being charmed." From this developed the idea in the use of the word to denote "being without control" or "wantonness" and "licentiousness."

With reference to sexual sins, the immorality of *aselgeia* is that the sex life is entirely uncontrolled. The passions are allowed to run riot and control the whole person, so that sex becomes the ruling aspect of the personality without regard for its real purposes. While not specifically stated, homosexuality, which is discussed next, may be included in *aselgeia*.

Homosexuality

According to D. S. Bailey (*Homosexuality and the Western Christian Tradition*), references to homosexuality in the Bible are almost nonexistent and many of those which have been traditionally so interpreted have another meaning. He refuses a homosexual interpretation of the Sodom account as a "superstitious inference from the awful character of the disaster." [3] Likewise, Bailey finds little evidence elsewhere in the Old Testament for homosexual acts. However, with regard to the Sodom account, while denying any sexual character to the approach and demand of the men at Lot's house, he fails to explain why Lot would attempt to satisfy their demand by giving his two virgin daughters for sexual purposes (cf. Gen. 19:8).

Of the three passages in the New Testament which Bailey considers, he finds only one (Rom. 1:26–27) to be an actual homosexual reference (p. 37). Each of these passages will here be reviewed briefly.

Romans 1:26–27.—"For this reason God gave them up to dishonorable passions. Their women exchanged natural relations for unnatural, and the men likewise gave up natural relations with women and were consumed with passion for one another, men committing shameless acts with men and receiving in their own persons the due penalty for their error."

These two verses fall within the context of a discussion on the depravity of man and its expressions by the apostle Paul. In verses 19 through 32, he points specifically at the perversion and failure of the Gentiles to receive the revelation of God. Beginning with verse 24, he gives a description of two classes of sins which mark the failure of Gentile pagan society to acknowledge God. The first group of sins is sexual and the second group, beginning with verse 28, is the antisocial list.

The sexual sins which Paul attacks are well documented in Greek and Roman literature of the times. Enslin observes: "In no other point of morals was the contrast between the teachings of Paul and the general habits and opinions of the Roman world more clearly seen than in this attitude toward homosexual love." [4] Plato and others refer approvingly to homosexual practices. [5]

The language used in these two verses is clearly homosexual; the reference is made to both males and females. Bailey thinks the female reference is ambiguous and could admit of a heterosexual interpretation, but this is not possible when the close connection between the two verses is recognized. The connecting adverb, "likewise," indicates that the description in verse 26 is intended to be a parallel of the thought of 27, except that one is female and the other male. Without verse 27, the reference in verse 26 to unnatural relations for women points rather clearly to something other than heterosexual relations.

Several charges are brought against the homosexual perversion in these verses. Homosexuality is the result of rebellion against God and the resulting dishonorable passions. Both verses bring the charge of an "unnatural" or "against nature" practice. Again the unbridled desire which consumes and distorts the whole person is denounced. Finally, the homosexual practice is described as a "shameful thing" which reduces one to complete degradation. The whole discussion is Paul's prime example of man's inner perverseness and sin.

Look briefly at verse 32. Here the apostle concludes that all the previously mentioned sins stand under the condemnation. For him the occurrence of these sins in society is completely reprehensible, but a further step of degradation is approval and acceptance without a sense of shame by the society itself. The very existence of these practices is self-indicting enough for society, but approval and pride in them is to render society hopeless.

First Corinthians 6:9.—"Do you not know that the unrighteous will not inherit the kingdom of God? Do not be deceived; neither the immoral, nor idolaters, nor adulterers, nor homosexuals." Two Greek terms are translated by the one English word "homosexuals" in the Revised Standard Version. The first of these literally means "effeminate." While Bailey doubts that either of the classes is necessarily invert, the RSV translators seem to have followed the thought of the list. There is little doubt that the second word refers to homosexuality, especially here, since both prostitutes and adulterers have already been mentioned.

With severity the Corinthian Christians were warned that such practices were not characteristic of those who inherit the kingdom of God. Those who are given to such practices stand in need of the redemptive grace of God. Sanctification of the person in marriage and sex involves the channeling of these relationships into fruitful and creative courses rather than those mentioned in this list.

Mention should be made here of the other appearance of this latter word in 1 Timothy 1:9. Those listed in this passage are said to stand also under the judgment of God in the law and in themselves oppose "sound doctrines." The homosexuals are listed with the prostitutes in 1 Timothy as in 1 Corinthians. There appears to have been great need for ethical instruction and prohibition in sexual matters in the environment of the early church.

The discussion of these perversions has more value than simply to outline the prohibitions with regard to sex; such discussion has value for arriving at a constructive theology of sex. To see on what basis these various practices and attitudes were condemned helps us to know on what basis virtue is to be established.

Otto Piper gives four virtues which are to be present in a proper sexual relationship: love, fidelity, accord with nature, and chastity.[6] These appear well established by a review of the charges made against the above aberrations.

Reduction of sexuality to a salable or simply usable item and detachment from the total personality is the destructive element in *porneia* (fornication). This stands in complete opposition to the expression of mutual love in which the whole person is surrendered to the other. The distance between the desire in *porneia* and the experience of *agape* is the distance of opposite poles. The unrecognized and insatiable hunger expressed in *porneia* is that of a person whose insecurity within himself and in his relationships has rendered him incapable of a valid *agape* experience.

Infidelity is the chief characteristic of *moicheia* (adultery). This flouting of fidelity has serious consequences for the Christian ideal. Piper has said that "infidelity degrades the value of what we possess in the fact of sex unity: it pays too little regard to the deep meaning of sex and the personal dignity of the other, and the final consequence is quite usually a disregard for, or a false estimation of the world, and a sense of contempt for mankind." [7] Then he makes the contrast by showing the character of fidelity. "Faithfulness has also a positive side. It consists in so ordering our lives that no other worldly interest takes a higher place than our interests for our consort."

Adultery is lack of commitment, which Jesus recognized in emphasizing the evil desire to be as serious as the act itself. In speaking of adultery both as an inner urge and its expression in divorce, he was assuming and implying the indispensable place of fidelity in the marital relationship.

Chastity as a virtue in sex is implied in the New Testament attack on *akatharsia* (uncleanness). Freedom from all kinds of sexual sins considered is included in the biblical idea of chastity. *Akatharsia* is the condition of life where chastity and sanctification are impossible. On the other hand, chastity is not a complete absence of sexual functioning by the person; rather it is a wholesome functioning within marriage which exalts the other virtues.

A virtue which Piper does not consider as such is self-control. To be sure, self-control is involved in some of the other virtues, but it is emphasized directly in New Testament writers. Paul especially recognized that there were those who would need to give attention to self-control in sexuality. For many the necessity of this would be before marriage, but for others it would continue into marriage.

A measure of self-control is indispensable where sexual adjustment needs to be made in marriage. *Aselgeia* (licentiousness) is the complete absence of such self-control which gives unbridled indulgence to every desire. As demonstrated above, the lack of control may express itself in numerous ways but the source of it is found in the interior of man (cf. Mark 7:22). Here, as with *akatharsia,* the ultimate of this virtue is not denial of sexuality but its proper expression.

There remains of Piper's suggested virtues "accord with nature" to be considered. Homosexuality is the assailant of this virtue, according to Romans 1:26–27. A sexual orientation "according to nature" would involve both the acceptance of bisexual creation and the desire for a fruitful union. Both of these factors are ignored in homosexuality. Still further, homosexuality is an indication that the person for some reason has had his sexuality short-circuited and it cannot become the intended expression of the whole person for a member of the opposite sex.

The positive value, then, of the study of these aberrations lies not only in the limits of prohibitions but sheds much light on the intention of God for human sexuality. It will be observed that the basis for these virtues is a prior commitment to God. This is especially so when it is realized that freedom from these sins cannot be guaranteed by laws or precise prohibitions; rather, freedom from them lies only in the person rightly related to God and properly oriented toward others.

Some of these sins lie wholly in the realm of misorientation, others, which once were considered only acts, Jesus laid bare to show their roots in inner misdirection. To consider these perversions is not to discredit sexuality from Christian personality and marriage. The propriety of complete abstention is explored in a later chapter.

6. Women in the New Testament

One of the most knotted problems of applying New Testament principles to husband-wife relationships is the apparent attitude toward women taken in some of the Epistles. The relatively recent assertion of women for rights and independence makes any vestige of male authority or female subordination seem completely out of place. On this basis many have discarded all such references in the New Testament as merely a reflection of an ancient society whose standards for the sexes have now given way to a different culture.

It will be our intention in this chapter and the next to examine the attitudes and passages about the relative status of wife to husband, to determine if valid principles remain for any concept of subordination in marriage.

The Position of Women Reflected in Ministries

Associations with women were frequent in the ministry of Jesus. Several women were among his most devoted followers; e.g., Mary and Martha, Mary Magdalene, the mother of James and Joseph, and others. Luke especially took cognizance of Jesus' ministry to women (widow with two mites, the "daughters of Jerusalem," and the woman with an issue).

The position of women, reflected in his contacts with them, was chiefly one of household service, which is in keeping with that reflected in the Mishnah and other Palestinian sources. Such examples as Peter's mother-in-law (cf. Mark 1:30 f.), women grinding at the mill (cf. Matt. 24:41), and the woman at the well (cf. John 4:7 ff.) show this. Motherhood, of course, is another aspect of the position revealed. A third aspect of this status is a quasi-recognition in religious service. It was this last aspect that Jesus encouraged in his ministry (cf. Luke 10:42 ff.; Matt. 26:12 f.).

The early Christian movement depended heavily on the efforts of women; especially was this true in the ministry of Paul. Acts, like its prologue Luke, gives emphasis to the ministry of women. Paul mentions in his Epistles several women who made contributions to his ministry or to the lives of the churches which he served. Several are named in the greeting of Romans 16:1 ff., and the entire chapter appears to have been a recommendation for the deaconess Phoebe (cf. also Phil. 4:2; Col. 4:15).

It becomes noticeable that as the Christian movement passed into the more Gentile and Diaspora world, women engaged more actively and directly in the ministry of the churches. Paul accepted and encouraged their help. However, when they became prominent and their conduct threatened the orderliness of worship, Paul reverted to his Jewish customs and attitudes about women.

The status of women in Paul's teaching does not appear uniformly consistent. This is again partially due to the variety of problems faced. Therefore, it is necessary to make a distinction between his theological concepts and his practical answers in such matters. His most detailed consideration of the status of women is 1 Corinthians 11:2–16. To understand Paul's position we will consider the passage at some length:

I commend you because you remember me in everything and maintain the traditions even as I have delivered them to you. But I want you to understand that the head of every man is Christ, the head of a woman is her husband, and the head of Christ is God. Any man who prays or prophesies with his head covered dishonors his head, but any woman who prays or prophesies with her head unveiled dishonors her head—it is the same as if her head were shaven. For if a woman will not veil herself, then she should cut off her hair; but if it is disgraceful for a woman to be shorn or shaven, let her wear a veil. For a man ought not to cover his head, since he is the image and glory of God; but woman is the glory of man. (For man was not made from woman, but woman from man. Neither was man created for woman, but woman for man.) That is why a woman ought to have a veil on her head, because of the angels. (Nevertheless, in the Lord woman is not independent of man nor man of woman; for as woman was made from man, so man is now born of woman. And all things are from God.) Judge for yourselves; is it proper for a woman to pray to God with her head uncovered? Does not nature itself teach you that for a man to wear long hair is degrading to him, but if a woman has long hair, it is her pride? For her hair is given to her for a covering. If any one is disposed to be contentious, we recognize no other practice, nor do the churches of God.

In this third section of 1 Corinthians (11:1 to 14:40), the apostle is dealing with disorders in public worship. Both Gentile and Jewish believers made up the Corinthian church, bringing with them a diversity of customs and backgrounds. This in itself, in so close a fellowship as the early church, would tend to generate problems. A further difficulty, it appears, was the fact that Paul wrote from his own Jewish background.

In following the thought of the passage, Paul's hope of convincing the Corinthian believers of his position was pinned on their willingness to accept and follow the body of teaching and practice he had attempted to make standard in every church (v. 2). For this he appeals to the *paradosis* here and "practice" in verse 16. Paul prefaces his practical advice with an attempt to show the theological significance of it. His appeal is to the principle of subordination, which obtains in divine as well as human unions. "Headship" here refers to order of office rather than a difference of personal importance. The three phrases of verse 3 must be taken together. That Paul is referring to married persons in this section is evident not only from the trend of discussion but the use of *aner* in contrast to *anthropos*.

Calvin understood this subordination as a necessary human arrangement: "Christ is the head of the man and of the woman without any distinction, because, as to that, there is no regard paid to male or female; but as regards external arrangement and political decorum, the man follows Christ and the woman the man, so that they are not upon the same footing, but, on the contrary, this inequality exists." [1]

Likewise, Paul viewed subordination as proper by inference from its existence in the Godhead. Beginning with verse 4, he shows how headship and subordination are symbolized even in the headdress and public appearance of men and women. His chief concern was with women, but he uses the male example to strengthen the necessity of women accepting their proper role. Robertson and Plummer summarize the intent of this verse as follows:

> Such conduct "dishonors his head" because covering it is a usage which symbolizes subjection to some visible superior, and in common worship the man has none: those who are visibly present are either his equals or inferiors. There is no reason for supposing that men at Corinth had been making this mistake in the congregation. The conduct would be improper for men but is mentioned in order to give point to the censure on women, who in this matter had been acting as men.[2]

The apparent conflict between the acceptance of women praying and prophesying and their prohibition in chapter 14:34–35 resolves itself when both are seen as an effort to prevent the women from assuming an equality with men.

Background considerations for both Paul and Corinth are extremely important for Paul's present discussion. Louis M. Epstein explains that "in the west that rule of modesty was not recognized, and St. Paul was much displeased over the fact." [3] It is quite possible that the propriety of the headdress of women which Paul assumed (without giving any explanation) was not as well accepted in Corinth as in the more Jewish milieu out of which Paul came. It is evident that the apostle assumed that to be without a veil was a mark of lewdness and insubordination for the wife.

Paul goes on to push their action to the extreme by saying that if the wives are going to ignore the appropriate symbol of subordination, why not dress as a prostitute? He returns in the last of verse 6 to show that the only way to prevent being identified with women of loose character is to be veiled.

By means of rabbinic exegesis, in which one word is grasped and an inference drawn from it, Paul explains why it is a shame for a man to have his head covered. "Image" is the key from which the apostle argues for the status of man, ignoring the fact that, in the Genesis 1:26 account, woman was included in the image. Linking the words "image" and "glory," the meaning of the latter approximates "reflection"; because man was made in the image of God, he is the "reflection" of him. Following this thought, the wife stands in reflected glory to the husband.

Parenthetically, in verses 8 and 9, Paul adds the argument of creation to strengthen his position of subjection for the wife. He uses "out of" and "account of" to emphasize man as the source and purpose of woman's creation. "Authority" in verse 10 (translated "veil") has been difficult to understand as shown by late Greek manuscripts, which read "covering" rather than "authority." However, in this context it seems best to accept the word *exousia* as a symbol of authority in the sense that woman is to approach God in her recognized place of subordination by having her veil. James Moffatt suggests the possibility that there was a Semitic term which meant both covering and authority.[4]

A second interpretive difficulty in this tenth verse is the reference to angels. Two of the most prominent interpretations are, first, it is a reference to the sin of Genesis 6:1–4; and second, it is a reference to the presence of angels in worship who would be shocked to see women without the veil. The previous reference to Genesis in this passage gives some weight to the first explanation (cf. Jude 6 and 2 Peter 2:4). However, since it is worship which is here being considered, and since there is a background of this thought in Jewish theology, the reference is probably to angels in the worship.

When we come to verses 11 and 12, it appears that Paul realizes he has pushed the subordination idea too far and begins now to balance it by showing the interdependence of the husband and wife. Here is Calvin's statement of this interdependence:

If they be separated, they are like the mutilated members of a mangled body. Let them, therefore, be connected with each other by the bond of mutual duty. When he says "in the Lord" he by this expression calls the attention of believers to the appointment of the Lord. The pious, on the other hand, acknowledge that the male sex is but half of the human race. Thus the man has no standing without the woman, for that would be the head severed from the body; nor has the woman without the man, for that were a body without a head. Let, therefore, the man perform to the woman the office of the head in respective of ruling her, and let the woman perform to the man the office of the body in respect of assisting him.[5]

Moffatt feels that this verse is the most lasting sentence of the discussion and that it really undermines the patriarchal theory which the apostle has been defending. Here Paul states the realization that although man was first to come into existence, it is through the woman that human existence is continued. God is the ultimate source of life, whether male or female.

In postscript style, verses 13 to 15 are added to the preceding arguments. After reasoning from subordination and creation, Paul here appeals to a sense of social propriety. In his words, the appeal "to what is proper" is added to "by nature." Paul assumed it as universal that men have short hair and women have long hair. This is one of the clearest pictures in the New Testament of the customs of dress which were considered appropriate.

Here in the last verse Paul, having exhausted his theological and social arguments, appeals to the universality of this position in all the other churches. Moffatt summarizes Paul's position for us as follows:

The paragraph exhibits the apostle hampered by ideas and customs of his age, anxious lest the religious freedom he proclaimed should be compromised by ardent souls, and at the same time half conscious that his own principle of Christian equality for sexes did not exactly square with the dress regulations which he felt bound to enforce, in his anxiety to prevent any of his own churches breaking loose from a tradition about God in public worship which had been adopted by the Jewish Christian communities.[6]

1 Corinthians 14:34–35

A more severe blow is given to the status of women when the apostle in this passage addresses other disorders in the church: "The women should keep silence in the churches. For they are not permitted to speak, but should be subordinate, as even the law says. If there is anything they desire to know, let them ask their husbands at home. For it is shameful for a woman to speak in church" (RSV).

The picture of woman's status given in this passage stands in apparent conflict with other insights, since here they are forbidden to pray. Moffatt, Robertson and Plummer, Craig and Short all agree that the extreme disorder caused by woman in the services prompted this sharp prohibition. It is to be expected that in Jewish churches the women would be more secluded and silent than those of Gentile character. Especially is this prohibition understandable in a church like Corinth, where ecstasy and disorder had almost precluded worship.

Paul bases his denial of the woman's freedom to speak on his understanding of the principle of subordination. The permission to pray or prophesy which was recognized earlier (11:4) was removed in these verses, because it was abused to the point of complete disorder. Some commentators suggest that a message of further disorder had been received by Paul in the time between the writing of the two passages. It is doubtful, therefore, that this pronouncement which addressed an extreme situation should be taken as a universal principle or used to assign a permanent status to women.

In a summary evaluation of Paul's attitude toward women, as stated in the Corinthian correspondence, it becomes obvious that his standard is very much the one of his day, as seen in a study on cultural backgrounds. Adhering strongly and sometimes quite strictly to the principle of subordination, he relegated women to a secondary place in society. However, within the framework of his understanding of grace, Paul seemed to become vaguely aware of a sense of equality which should exist between fellow believers. He still insisted that wives should accept their place of respect and subjection to their husbands. It is principally in Paul's theology and occasionally in situations where he applied this theology that he enunciated truths and worked out principles which were not limited to customs of the first century. There remains still another Pauline passage to be considered.

1 Timothy 2:8–15

I desire . . . also that women should adorn themselves modestly and sensibly in seemly apparel, not with braided hair or gold or pearls or costly attire but by good deeds, as befits women who profess religion. Let a woman learn in silence with all submissiveness. I permit no woman to teach or to have authority over men; she is to keep silent. For Adam was formed first, then Eve; and Adam was not deceived, but the woman was deceived and became a transgressor. Yet woman will be saved through bearing children, if she continues in faith and love and holiness, with modesty.

The "peaceableness" (v. 8) is to be matched by the modesty of women in public worship services. This section addresses itself to the kind of dress and conduct which is most acceptable to believing women. Parallels with 1 Peter 3:1–7 are plainly evident, and in this passage also it is specifically wives who are addressed.

All that follows in verses 9 and 10 serves to make explicit the meaning of "seemly apparel" or "orderly adornment." The first qualifying characteristics of "orderly adornment" are *aidous* and *sophrosunas*. Locke says of the words:

Aidous—that shamefastness which shrinks from overpassing the limits of womanly reserve and modesty. *Sophrosunas*—that habitual inner self-government which with its constant reign of all the passions

and desires which would hinder temptation from arising, or at all
events arise in such strength as should overbear the checks and barriers
which *aidous* opposed to it.[7]

The negative side of the adornment has discounted the value
of jewelry and attractive ornaments, including expensive clothing,
which were associated with moral looseness in ancient societies.
This is the same attitude toward wearing apparel as expressed
in 1 Peter 3:5. The exaltation of good works and the disparagement of physical attractiveness is paralleled in Euripides, who
makes Andromache say, "This is the love charm—woman, 'tis not
beauty, that witcheth bridegrooms, nay, but nobleness." [8]
The force of the last of verse 10 is to point out that the
standard for those who profess discipleship is different from those
who make no profession. As Calvin says, "for undoubtedly the
dress of a virtuous and godly woman must differ from that of a
strumpet." [9] A woman's adornment then must be appropriate to
her religious profession, and for the believer this is accomplished
through an emphasis on good works.
The fabric of society which clothed the early church becomes
more apparent through the course of these verses. Subjection,
which is called for in verses 11 and 12, is not equalized by a
command to the husbands, as in other passages considered. There
is envisioned here a kind of godly "quietness" that has a "peaceful" quality about it. Yet women are excluded here from leading
in worship.
It may well be as Scott suggests, "Perhaps in the present passage
the word 'teach' is taken in the technical sense of making a public
set address." [10] The passage is made more tolerable and understandable by reference to "lording it over men." The context of
this advice could well be a situation in which Christian women
were flouting the freedom realized as fellow believers with their
husbands. Using the word which has a "peacefulness" connotation
as opposed to the one which means simple silence further suggests
a need for orderliness in public services. It cannot be denied,

however, that a subservient attitude, for women, is enjoined in this passage.

Here again we meet the argument from creation as the basis for the wife's submission in verses 13–15. Only here there is added the argument from the sequence of man's fall in the Garden of Eden. The wife is given the responsibility for the initiation of the sin and, in fact, nothing is said about man's part. An inference is made that women are not to teach, because of their susceptibility to being deceived. While this type of reasoning may not commend itself to present thinkers, it was standard rabbinic reasoning to draw such inferences from the archetypal story.

"She will be saved" in verse 15 presents some difficulty of meaning. It has been suggested that this may refer to salvation by childbearing alone. Or again, taking a clue from the preceding "Eve" reference, childbearing has redeemed woman, because through it came the Saviour, thus reversing the effect of the Garden experience. E. F. Scott suggests a more acceptable view when he says that "it seems best to take the Greek preposition and the phrase 'through child-bearing' not in its usual sense of 'by means of' but as denoting a condition. 'She will be saved even though she must bear children.' " [11]

Thus, being denied a prominent place in public meetings, woman's place is in the sphere of the home. The value of this place is enhanced by the attributes which follow, "in faith and love and holiness with modesty." The most shining truth of this passage is its recognition of the sacred calling of godly motherhood.

Are there any lasting principles operative in these apostolic answers in 1 Corinthians and 1 Timothy? To be sure, in specific directions of dress, there is the portrayal of a culture and customs which even in itself was not uniform and which has varied widely since that time. Included in this culture of first-century Judaism was an extremely subservient attitude toward women who were yet, in cruder moments, thought of as men's possessions. This does not mean, however, that no value remains in these passages.

In fact, one element which at first may seem to be simply a cultural reflection is one which can remain valid, if viewed in its proper perspective in Christian marriage. Subordination in marriage, conceived of as simply the assignment of roles and not the status of the sexes, is not only biblically sound but does not need to be an oppressive condition.

The next chapter considers this principle at greater length, but it is well to note here that in Corinth especially Paul was aware of an underlying issue. He associated with this concept its necessary corollary in the ideal of interdependence. Not just in origin and biologically, as the apostle notes, but by the very nature of marriage as a relationship there exists always an interdependence. Neither the husband nor the wife is to live without consideration of the other person. This is not to be expressed in a clinging, oversolicitous way but rather in mutual respect for the needs and desires of the other. Husband and wife become responsible for one another.

One salient principle is operative in all these passages and could not but be applied in times of the culture in which it was written. What was actually being advised and pleaded for was a sense of Christian modesty. It takes little observation to recognize that what may be perfect modesty in one culture may be the dress of prostitutes in another. In the United States there has been an amazing change of dress in an extremely short span of years. Paul was assuming and advising on the basis that a Christian is responsible to live decently in this society. In most cultures responsibility for decency is placed more heavily on women than men.

Perhaps one of the first principles of modesty is the avoidance of extremes in either direction. Any attempt to take specific directions of dress from one society and follow them in another results in confusion, but the wisdom of Christian modesty is demanded in every society. The New Testament emphasis on the attractiveness of the inner character in the life of a godly woman is never out of place.

Another virtue for which the passages plead is propriety. By this we mean a conservative exercise of one's freedom. Its lack was exemplified in the early church by women whose conduct was such as to disrupt the services of the church. This, like modesty, may vary in its expression, depending upon the standards of society and environment. Thus it demands that the Christian determine that which is proper in personal conduct in whatever society may exist. Impropriety, which is often associated with arrogance, does not make Christianity attractive nor does it bespeak a life submitted to God.

These, then, are some of the lasting values upon which the specific advice of the above passages was given. It will be left to the next chapter, where the place of man is considered, to assess more clearly the roles of husband and wife. The necessity of determining these lasting values and principles is a delicate task. It would be easier to discard the entire thought of the passages or to rigidly demand their application *verbatim*. To seek the underlying principle for Christian living commends itself more clearly as the New Testament method.

7. Roles of Husband and Wife

This is obviously less a man's world today than when Jesus and his first followers faced it. The assertion of women for equal rights does not entirely account for this; there is no longer the need for the male assertion as the physical protector of the family (especially the women) from harm as in primitive societies. Women are no longer entirely, if at all, dependent upon men economically.

Inevitably, with the changing of personal and social needs, the *roles* of men and women would be affected, even in marriage. However, this is not to say that the roles of husband and wife must now, or at any time for that matter, become completely identical in order for each to achieve the status of a real person. There still remains the physical and biological differences between male and female. Our own society has confused the liberty of each to achieve selfhood with achieving identical roles.

It will be the hope of this chapter to find a theological basis for husband and wife roles which is consistent with a Christian view of personhood.

The Status of Men

Little explicit information is found in the New Testament as to the status of man, but the reflections of his position can be seen. Jesus accepted the social status of men and women as he found it; he was not a social reformer per se. Commerce and government were largely confined to the sphere of men as depicted in the Gospels, and social life was centered chiefly in their interest

71

as well (cf. Matt. 13:44–45; 22:2 ff.; 9:9 ff.). They were not only the protectors but also the masters of the home, commanding respect and service from the rest of the household (cf. Luke 11:5 ff.; Mark 13:35 ff.).

Governing religious bodies were composed of men where the minute questions of faith and practice became their province of decision. To none of these stations did Jesus object except as they were used in arrogant pride or in exploitation of others. Rather, by the very nature of his ethic, the inequalities of social status were adjusted in an atmosphere of outgoing concern. This picture of male ascendancy is in keeping with that given us in the Mishnah and other Palestinian sources (cf. Kethuboth 4:4–5).

With Paul, as with Jesus, an exact comparative statement of the position of men to women is difficult. Men's status can only be inferred from the position of women. Paul expected man to be the head of the family as the leader of the social unit. Men were expected to provide discipline, but this was to be done with understanding (cf. Col. 3:21). From 1 Corinthians 11:2–16, we have seen that customs of dress were quite distinct for the sexes. It was disgraceful for a man to be attired in woman's manner of dress. It is implied that it is a disgrace for him to take the station of a woman.

The Pastorals also stress that man is to be the head and ruler of the family, making this station prerequisite to officeholding in the church (cf. 1 Tim. 3:3,4,12). At the same time, there was in the ethic of Paul an antidote to this male superiority, but it did not begin to take effect until centuries later. On the other hand, Paul struck upon a principle of theology which is helpful in understanding the roles of husband and wife: it is the principle of subordination.

Subordination

Theologically speaking, even in the Godhead subordination exists. The relationship of Jesus, the Son, to God the Father is pictured as one of subordination. When Paul implies and states this he is not subtracting from the person of Jesus. The Son's subordination to the Father is expressed in his filial obedience and confidence, as is seen in 1 Corinthians 15:24–28: -

Then comes the end, when he delivers the kingdom to God the Father after destroying every rule and every authority and power. For he must reign until he has put all his enemies under his feet. The last enemy to be destroyed is death. "For God has put all things in subjection under his feet." But when it says, "All things are put in subjection under him," it is plain that he is excepted who put all things under him. When all things are subjected to him, then the Son himself will also be subjected to him who put all things under him, that God may be everything to every one.

Commenting on this concept, P. T. Forsyth points out that "obedience is not conceivable without some form of subordination. Yet in His very obedience the Son was co-equal with the Father; the Son's yielding will was no less divine than the Father's exigent will." [1]

James Stewart observes that "the very phrase 'the God and Father of our Lord Jesus Christ' envisages a relationship of dependence." [2]

As we have seen above, Paul states plainly that the Father is the head of Christ (cf. 1 Cor. 11:3). The apostle also uses this idea to state that the believer is subordinate to Christ, as in 1 Corinthians 3:23: "You are Christ's; and Christ is God's."

In addition to Christ's subordination to the Father's being one of obedience, it is characterized by a voluntary nature. Hence, there is no hint of inequality of Father and Son, except as the Son subjects himself to the limitations of human life in the redemptive life and death. It is in every sense a voluntary subordination as Jesus surrenders himself to the subordinate position by accepting his earthly humiliation: "Therefore God has highly exalted him and bestowed on him the name which is above every name, that at the name of Jesus every knee should bow, in heaven and on earth and under the earth, and every tongue confess that Jesus Christ is Lord, to the glory of God the Father" (Phil. 2:9–

11). Everywhere Paul asserts the full deity of Jesus (cf. Col. 1:19; 2:9; Rom. 1:7).

The next step in the principle of subordination is that of the believer to Christ. Here the relationship is not the same as between the Father and the Son, since it is not a voluntary inequality of status. Subordination on the part of the believer is that which acknowledges the lordship of Christ. The believer is more dependent on Christ and subordination, therefore, is more to be expected than in the relationship of the Son to the Father. This whole theology of marriage is based ultimately on a subordination of the participating believer to Christ.

Subordination extends to the entire body of believers as the church (cf. Eph. 5:24). In fact, it is the goal of redemption to subject all things under Christ. "He has put all things under his feet and has made him the head over all things for the church." From the subjection learned in the believer relationship, it is to be extended to the various human relationships.

E. G. Selwyn, in *The First Epistle of St. Peter*, discovers a common view of subordination which runs through 1 Peter, Romans, 1 Timothy, and Titus. Romans is chiefly concerned with subjection to civil powers (cf. 13:1–7), while 1 Peter broadens the horizon to include "every human establishment" (2:13). Following this verse are a number of applications to various examples of subordination. In regard to subjection in the civil and social realm, however, the church found it necessary to define the limits of subjection to that which could be termed "in the Lord."

Within the Christian community the principle of subordination was necessary for the orderly functioning of the group (cf. 1 Peter 5:5; Heb. 13:17). Since one office or gift was not considered to be above another (cf. 1 Cor. 12:14–26), this was not, theoretically, a recognition of superior and inferior positions; rather it was a recognition of the necessity of leaders and the inherent exercise of "authority." Wherever orderly functioning evoked the exercise of subordination, it was expected to be voluntary and in an atmosphere of *agape* (cf. Eph. 4:15–16).

Selwyn has discovered a common source, known as a "household code," which contains the teaching that in the marriage relationship the principle of subordination was applied in the New Testament.[3] Its repeated occurrence in Ephesians, Colossians, 1 Peter, 1 Timothy, and Titus support this conclusion. In these formulae for family relationships some common elements included are exhortation for the wife to subject herself to her husband, modesty in dress, love of husbands for wives, and considerateness within the family. The Ephesian passage has already been noted, and since the passage in 1 Peter is one of the most extensive it is considered here:

1 Peter 3:1–7

Likewise you wives, be submissive to your husbands, so that some, though they do not obey the word, may be won without a word by the behavior of their wives, when they see your reverent and chaste behavior. Let not yours be the outward adorning with braiding of hair, decoration of gold, and wearing of robes, but let it be the hidden person of the heart with the imperishable jewel of a gentle and quiet spirit, which in God's sight is very precious. So once the holy women who hoped in God used to adorn themselves and were submissive to their husbands, as Sarah obeyed Abraham, calling him lord. And you are now her children if you do right and let nothing terrify you (RSV).

As noted above, this passage is an application of the principle stated in 2:13, "subject yourselves to every human institution because of the Lord." Here "likewise" aligns this passage as a parallel to 2:18, where slaves and masters are concerned. This is not the subjection of woman to man but that of a *wife* to *her own husband*. Selwyn sees this in the adjective *idios:* "This word delivers the passage from any charge of inculcating the 'inferiority' of women to men, and shows that subordination is one of function, within the intimate circle of the home. St. Peter's teaching implies that every institution must have a head for practical purposes, and in the home this should be the husband." [4]

Elmer Homrighausen sees the Christian intent in the sentence when he says: "There is nothing said here about inferiority and

superiority; what is maintained is rather the fact that the relationship which exists between husband and wife is to be respected and
submitted to, so long as it does not run counter to Christian
convictions." [5]

Also what D. S. Bailey says of the Ephesian passage is equally
applicable here: "He is concerned, not with woman's legal or
social status, but the operation within the 'one-flesh' union of a
principle of subordination which finds expression wherever community exists, although its range is indeed almost universal." [6]

Selwyn claims that the phrase "though they do not obey" shows
that Peter had more in view than simply the wives of unbelieving
husbands. This is true of the general principle first stated, but
Peter limits the application of the principle to its effectiveness in
a Christian-pagan home. "The word" in verse 1 can be understood as referring to the word of the gospel, while "without a
word" (article "the" absent) refers simply to an absence of verbal
persuasion. Paul uses *kerdaino* (win) to refer to making converts
(cf. 1 Cor. 9:19–22) and that which will "convert" is the "manner
of life" (*anastrophen*) which is described as being "in fear and
reverent" (v. 2). This is not fear of the husband but reverence
before God. Here is the recognition, emphasized by both Paul and
Peter, that Christian conduct does affect public and private opinion.

Beginning with verse 3, Peter gives further explanation to the
"manner of life" which is proper and effective in making converts
of unbelieving husbands. The adornments here mentioned were
referred to by Isaiah in his satire (cf. 3:18–24).

Selwyn observes, "Fine dress is symptomatic of luxurious living
in the description of Dives in Luke 16:19, and of the wicked city
in Revelation 17:4, and it is associated with sexual sin in Apoc.
Pet. 9." [7]

Having discounted the adornment approach, he turns to present
the real person as his concern and uses a thought parallel to
Paul's "inner man" (Eph. 3:16). The emphasis is ethical more
than theological. It is not in physical attractiveness but in meek-
ness, incorruptibility, quietness, and preciousness before God that

Christian beauty is beheld. According to the standards of his age, Peter is pleading for modesty.

The next two verses (5 and 6) are a continuation of the argument for modesty by reference to Jewish matriarchal history, especially to Sarah. "Subjection" was the adornment which made these models acceptable to their husbands. "Subordination, active well-doing, and serenity are the three qualities here inculcated in ancient example," notes Selwyn.[8] The reference to becoming "children" of these ancient matrons is that of becoming like them or patterns of their practice. It is still evident in this passage that the author felt the pattern of primitive culture was right in imposing a "subjection" upon the wife. Still this does not destroy the validity of sensible subordination in husband-wife relationships.

With verse 7, the author turns to give a word of admonition to believing husbands. Various suggestions have been made as to the content of the "knowledge" recommended, such as spiritual enlightenment, awareness of the wife's needs, or even instruction in marriage such as is given at present. No doubt all these should be included as an understanding of womanhood, but this knowledge must extend also to a concept of the marriage relationship which would rightly assess the matter of subordination in Christian marriage.

"Vessel" (*skevos*) in this verse does not mean "wife" or "simply chattel" (contra Bigg); rather, Selwyn makes a valid comparison in saying, "The 'vessel' here thought of is the whole personality of the wife, regarded as a representative of her sex."[9] Also, the use of the comparative "weaker" supports the conclusion that "person" is referred to and intimates that the husband is also a "vessel."

Possession of this "knowledge" is exemplified in the "honor" bestowed. An equivalence of position is implied in the phrase "joint heirs of the grace of life," which must be acknowledged in the matter of subordination. Again we are reminded that subordination is a principle of the husband-wife relationship, not a statement of their relative positions before God.

The Apostle ends his exhortation with the observation that if the husband and wife do not live harmoniously together, it will result in an undesirable spiritual condition in which prayer will be unavailing and perhaps impossible.

Out of the various passages and ideas considered, the loftiest statement of the principle of subordination is that which is found in Ephesians. Cast in the symbol of a head-body unity of which Christ and the church are archetypes, both husband and wife have their respective places. The atmosphere of love and sacrifice, in which the subjection is ameliorated, makes this an expression of reciprocal love. These same admonitions are given in Colossians 3:18, where the imperative "submit yourselves" for the wife is followed by "love your wives" for the husband. The entire reproof is made an ethic of believers by the words "as is [appropriate] in the Lord."

Paul draws the husband-wife subordination from the eternal order of Father-Son subordination in 1 Corinthians 11. Here, among the disorders of worship, Paul warns the women not to conduct themselves in such a way that they appear to reject the authority of their husbands. The appeal is made to their sense of Christian propriety and modesty.

Subordination has gotten out of the strictly Christian atmosphere in the admonition of Peter. However, the motive of subordination of the believing wife in this instance is that she may thereby win her husband to faith. Comparison is also made to the more fitting character of the appeal of subordination than to the appeal of apparel.

A very similar comparison of adornment versus subordination is made in the Pastorals. Here subordination has become a rule to be observed and the previous lofty atmosphere of the doctrine has somewhat receded. The attitude prevailed that resort to jewelry and adornment stood in opposition to godly subordination. It is evident that the fear of Christian women's becoming or being identified with prostitutes or unbelievers was great.

It cannot be disputed that an androcentricity of the first-century culture certainly affected and determined much of the subordination teaching. The recognition of this fact, however, does not destroy all validity of the principle inculcated; rather, the understandings of the appropriate roles of husband and wife, along with the recognition of the status in the family, are valid, especially in an atmosphere of love and with the application of a distinctly Christian ethic. D. S. Bailey has well summarized this Christian principle:

In marriage as a natural ordinance we find a unilateral subordination; male and female have been so constituted with reference to one another that their relative status can only be expressed in terms of "headship" of the man and the "subjection" of woman. This does not of course mean (as so many think) that woman is inferior to man and somehow lower in the scale of being, though it does imply that she is radically different from him.[10]

Subordination, then, is the recognition of the appropriate roles of husbands and wives to which we now give our attention.

The primary and supreme command in the husband's role is "love your wife" (Eph. 5:25 ff.; Col. 3:18; 1 Cor. 7:3–4). This command determines all other relationships and functions which are present in Christian marriage and leads to sacrifice and care for the wife. The husband is to be cognizant of the needs and desires of the wife (cf. 1 Peter 3:7), recognizing that his existence is bound up with hers (cf. 1 Cor. 11:11–12). It is in the concept "as Christ loved the church" that the measure of the husband's love is found. He is to be the sacrificial agent with whom no cost is too great to pay to express his love for his wife.

The "cross" principle in married love must exist for marriage to be a truly one-flesh union. If it does exist, then whatever headship or authority the husband exercises will be "on behalf of" and with concern for the wife.

Within this environment of love the husband has the responsibility and duty of performing the functions of the head in a "one-flesh" union. In light of the New Testament concept of equal

accessibility to God of every believer there can be no assertion of
male superiority in this role. It is only assigned in the necessity of
a functioning head for every unit of society and is dependent
upon the voluntary subjection of the wife. Biblically, the basis
of it stems from the order of creation and the recognition of the
differences in the sexes; e.g., the different functions of male and
female in procreation. This differentiation of the physical makeup
and, to some extent, psychological structure cannot be ignored.
The term "head" itself suggests a vital dependence upon the
"body" whom it serves.

The primary task of the wife, as stressed in the New Testament,
is that of accepting her role in subordination. Under the conditions outlined in the role of the husband, this is not a form of
slavery; rather, it is a recognition of roles within a working social
unit. A sense of equality does exist in a proper "one-flesh" union,
but there is no place for a *demand* of equality in every respect
to be made by the wife, just as there is no place for a *demand*
of subordination to be made by the husband.

Certainly there are limits to the application of the principle
of subordination. For example, as Forsyth observes, it cannot go
to the limits of renouncing Christ at the demand of the husband.
When the culture of the New Testament has been viewed, as it has
in the preceding chapters, what remains of subordination is clearly
seen to be voluntary. The concepts of one-flesh and head-body
unity leave no room for an external imposition of subordination.
The wife voluntarily accepts her role for the well-being of the
relationship, not because she fears a tyrant husband. It was not
by accident that the middle form, "submit yourselves," was used
in reference to subordination.

Another emphasis of the wife's role concerns her care in
modesty. The New Testament writers looked with great suspicion
on seductive powers of women. It is highly important that the
dress and adornment of the wife be in keeping with the modest
customs of the time and culture. The quality of modesty included

a tenderness and understanding spirit which would furnish attractiveness for the husband.

The role of the wife is highly important in the domestic tranquility of the home. The status of women in the first century allowed this function to be emphasized. The biblical account of man-woman creation makes the companion feature of the wife role prominent. In addition to this, motherhood enhanced her role as wife, not only in the sense of bearing children, but also in providing a spiritual environment for their development.

The roles of husband and wife then are different from the simple status of man and woman in society. The roles of husband and wife in marriage are both distinct and yet complementary. By their very nature these roles cannot be legislated nor fulfilled under coercion, for even the exercise of the authority granted to a husband depends upon a life committed to God so that the authority will not be usurped. The relational character of these assigned roles suggests that the amount of authority or subordination within a given union may vary in intensity with the demands of the particular partners or circumstances. Each must not only accept his or her role in marriage but must recognize the role assigned to the partner. If thus accepted and recognized each should be able to find his or her place in a happy one-flesh union.

8. Dealing with Conflicts

Inherent in the marriage relationship is the element of conflict.[1] With this statement David Mace voices one of the most poignant realities of marriage. Not only the intensity and intimacy of the marriage relationship but also the fact that two distinct personalities coalesce into one makes the probability of conflict very high. The incidence of divorce in nearly all societies is indicative of the proportions of some of these conflicts.

To be sure the basic disturbance is often quite different from its expression. However, there are certain areas which naturally furnish more opportunity for conflict than others. The New Testament is not a casebook on marital adjustments; yet, some of the areas of conflict are referred to and some principles for resolving them are given. Three areas especially can be pointed out as recognized by the New Testament, namely, religion, in-laws, and sexual compatibility.

Religious Conflicts in Marriage

Most pressing religious conflicts which early Christians faced were those of marriages between believers and unbelievers. Should a believer marry an unbeliever? Should a believer continue in marriage with an unbeliever? Can a believer win an unbeliever in marriage? Such questions as these plagued the minds of early Christians when suddenly they found Christianity standing in sharp contrast to the pagan society of their former life.

The advisability of a marriage between a believer and an unbeliever is doubtful. New Testament theology and ethics would not encourage the establishment of such a union. For one thing, it is demonstrated in the Gospels that Jesus demanded complete allegiance of those who would be his followers. Again, in Pauline theology the "in Christ" position of the believer is the supreme reality of life. The believer becomes a part of Christ and Christ dwells in him, so that when he becomes a participant in a one-flesh union *he is united as a believer.*

The spiritual dimension of life which the believer experiences cannot be shared by the unbeliever. Hence, here is an area where there could be no communion in the one-flesh union. A union which cannot express itself in spiritual fellowship is seriously impaired.

The impairment extends further to the ethic which would determine the moral decisions of the union, since in such a marriage they could not be wholly that of a believer. Forsyth points out the necessity of such an ethic by saying, "Christian ethic is not possible without a common Christian faith; and for such faith there is no other ethic." [2]

A lack of fellowship was Paul's concern in forbidding union of believers and unbelievers. He stated that they be not yoked with a different kind (cf. 2 Cor. 6:14). This word was used to show an inequality. There is the strong suggestion of "a different kind" in the use of this word. "Do not be mismated with unbelievers. For what partnership have righteousness and iniquity? Or what fellowship has light with darkness?" The apostle reflects this same attitude when he gives permission to the believing widow to marry but "only in the Lord" (1 Cor. 7:39).

Some of the purposes and functions of marriage may occur in a union of a believer with a nonbeliever. However, the fulfilment of the New Testament ideals for marriage would be extremely difficult and some, impossible. It is striking that so much attention has been given to marriage of divorced persons in biblical studies but very little to marriage of believers and unbelievers. There is as much or more incongruity between the New Testament ideal and actual practice in the latter case as in the former. Spiritual compatability was one of the main emphases of New Testament writers.

Still another aspect of the marriage of believer with unbeliever exists. Once such a marriage has been contracted the question arises whether it should be continued. Although this marriage cannot be entirely a "one-flesh" union, there is no encouragement to dissolve such a union. It is Paul's advice that if the unbeliever is agreeable, no sin is inherent in continuing the union (cf. 1 Cor. 7:12). This is especially recognized with reference to children, of whom Paul speaks as being legitimate, in such a union (cf. 1 Cor. 7:14). He seems to assume that an attempt will be made to win the unbeliever but he does not press the point (cf. 1 Cor. 7:16). On the other hand, Peter gives the wives very specific directions for winning their spouses to the faith (cf. 1 Peter 3:1 f.). It has been observed that this is to be done by manner of living rather than by a discourse of words.

Paul faces the prospect that the spouse cannot be won. In this case he gives preference to the Christian's possessing the grace to keep peace over the doubtful prospect of the unbeliever's conversion (cf. 1 Cor. 7:15). If the peace of the home is destroyed by the believer's insistence of maintaining the union, freedom should be granted to the unbeliever. The dissolution of a union in these circumstances should not lead to a feeling of judgment on the part of the believer. No place, however, is given to the believer to initiate separation. Unless insisted on by the unbeliever, the bond is not to be disturbed (cf. 1 Cor. 7:13).

Peace, according to Paul, is a necessary characteristic of the Christian life in marriage, as in all other relationships. In his discussion of this problem the apostle was dealing with believers who were questioning their status with unbelieving partners. The alternatives offered were wise and can still be considered with great profit.

The importance of peace which Paul urges is demonstrated in the effect of conflict upon religious and marital life. Earlier, sanctification was pointed out as a purpose of both marriage and sexuality. The New Testament view of marriage demands a spiritual atmosphere if the totality of a "one-flesh" union is to be realized. Both Paul and Peter expected that husbands and wives would devote themselves singly and together in prayer (cf. 1 Cor. 7:5; 1 Peter 3:7).

Another of the Christian principles which is enhanced by a spiritual atmosphere in the union is forgiveness. Love (*agape*) does its creative work in providing forgiveness in human life. David Mace points out the evident necessity of this atmosphere when he says, "The truth is that the whole fellowship of marriage is ultimately based on forgiveness. Two people unable to forgive could not endure to live together as a married couple." [3] Later he observes, "how effectively can the husband and wife, in their intimately shared life, confess their faults to each other and help and encourage each other to overcome them!" [4] Forgiveness is involved in the ability to accept the negative side of the marriage partner.

Greater opportunity rarely offers itself to exercise real forgiveness than in the marriage union. The person who is able or has learned to forgive in marriage has certainly developed along the lines of true sanctification.

On the other hand, growth of the spiritual life of partners may be thwarted and the religious life impeded if conflicts are allowed to grow without consideration. The fact that conflict is inherent in marriage is not a license for it to exist and flourish. Sexual abstinence, even for purposes of prayer, may result in marital conflict and even temptation if mutual consent and consideration to each other's needs are not given (cf. 1 Cor. 7:5).

Prayer itself may be impossible in a union where husbands do not exercise the love and consideration due their wives (cf. 1 Cor. 3:7). Bigg explains that "the two cannot join in prayer, as they ought to do, for a blessing on their married life, if there is injustice between them." [5] When human relationships, especially marriage, are disrupted by conflicts, invariably the ability to have a wholesome relationship with God is seriously impeded. Marriage

then offers one of life's finest opportunities for the development
of Christian personality. When this development is impeded by religious conflict, the Christian must face the alternatives and
seek that which will be most redemptive for the lives of both
partners.

The problem of religious conflict can be as acute an any experienced in the marriage relationship. There are now more
problems than that of believer and nonbeliever marriages. On
the one side, the spread and diversity of Christian and religious
groups offer a multiplication of opportunities for conflict in interfaith marriages. On the other side, the spreading cosmopolitanism
and amalgamation of cultures and religions have increased the
probability of interfaith marriages. The principles which have
been reviewed above can provide answers for these tensions
as well.

No area of conflict restricts itself to that particular sphere.
Religious conflicts generally involve the families of the couple
as well as themselves. Thus we are led directly into the area of
in-law relationships which we are to discuss next. While for
purposes of discussion we may compartmentalize these conflicts
into labeled areas, rarely do they exist in such isolation in actual
relationships. If we have found principles which help in dealing
with religious conflicts, they may also be beneficial to in-law
problems.

Problems with In-Laws

Among the relationships of family, that of husband and wife
takes precedence over all others for adults. The fact of a man and
woman united in one flesh makes that union the most intimate
and complete that is humanly possible. Even parent-child relationships do not possess the same mutuality nor the permanent
intimacy of a one-flesh union. In fact, the establishment of a one-
flesh union demands some severance of parent-child relationships
in biblical thought.

The most relevant biblical statement which concerns in-law

problems is that of Genesis 2:24, quoted in Mark 10:4: "Therefore a man leaves his father and his mother and cleaves to his wife, and they become one flesh." This "leaving" of parents and "cleaving" to a wife (or husband) emphasizes both the completeness of the one-flesh union and its supremacy over other relationships. Therefore, the severance of these other relationships is necessary to the degree that they no longer maintain a primacy.

Failure to recognize this primacy of the marriage relationship is attested to by the large number of in-law problems which threaten or destroy marriage. Added to this lack of understanding is the inability of many adults to sever or place secondary their earlier family relationships. A wholesome marriage relationship demands that both the husband-wife relationship and the former family relationships find their proper place in the thinking and feeling of the marriage partners. The in-law side of the problem must be considered.

The biblical wholistic concept of personality includes those attachments which a man or woman retains from previous experience. The Hebrew concept of family accepted those who married into the family as integral parts of the unit (*mishpachah*). Marriage was thought of as a cementing of two previously unattached families. Hence, while in the one-flesh union the parental ties were severed, there remained secondary relationships with the family from which the partners came and into which they married.

The New Testament concept of marriage does not abrogate the continuance of these secondary relationships. In fact, the wider implications of that concept reveal the need for and possibility of maintaining good in-law relationships. The consideration and mutual appreciation of a happy relational union may well extend to the attachments which either of the partners possesses in family ties. Mace describes this as a goal: "The grafting together of two families is great gain for all concerned. In-law relationships can become as strong and deep as the bonds of natural kinship. Surely Christian people will make this, and nothing less, their constant aim." [6]

Good in-law relationships depend ultimately on the orientation of the personalities involved. Evelyn Millis Duvall, in a study of contemporary American in-law relationships, finds a number of reasons for appreciation and love for in-laws. Some of the more prominent ones are the recognition of in-laws in rearing the partner loved and providing help in times of need.[7] Regardless of their expression, valid bases for good in-law relations will be sought for in a Christian marriage.

One of the highest frequencies of marital discord is in this area. The very presence of myriad mother-in-law jokes attests to an almost universal tension at this point. Mace explains something of the problem when he says:

This "leaving and cleaving" is one of the poignant yet inevitable human experiences. Between parent and child, as the child grows, deep bonds of mutual attachment are forged. Superficially, these are broken as the child matures. But they are not broken at deeper levels. All parents, however bad, invest something of themselves in their children.[8]

The problems of marriage are often multiplied or sometimes actually created by parents who are not willing to give up their investment. Thus, one of the major tasks of a Christian marriage is the seeking of a basis for satisfactory in-law relationships. Yet how really does this area offer opportunity for the expression of the determined goals in marriage.

The New Testament principle, which is the beginning point for solving in-law problems, is the recognition of the primacy of the marriage relationship between husband and wife. The ability to recognize and achieve this primacy depends on the maturity and adequacy of the couple. The initiative must be taken by each. Having established this primacy, it is then desirable for the couple to enjoy the secondary relationships with the families of both.

Not infrequently the problems of in-law conflict affect the marriage in other areas as well. If one marriage partner is resentful of the demand of the other partner for a primary relationship in the union, that one may retaliate in a withdrawal from communication or expression of love. Quite often, sexual disharmony results from such family resentments. This was noted by Tashman in *The Marriage Bed*.[9] Thus, we come to the other area of marital conflict which is reflected in New Testament writings.

Sexual Compatibility in Marriage

It has been discussed above that sexual intercourse is the physical and symbolic basis in the establishment of a "one-flesh" union. The importance of sexual compatibility is acknowledged by New Testament writers, especially as a demonstration of the kind of love and mutual commitment which is involved in marriage. Otto Piper says of this love in relation to sex: "It is not a supplement merely to the sex relationship properly so called, but an impulse which gives a new direction to the whole of sexual life." [10]

Marriage commitment is expressed in the mutual exchange of the authority of bodies, or as Paul states it: "The wife hath not power of her own body, but the husband: and likewise also the husband hath not power of his own body, but the wife" (1 Cor. 7:4). Thus the propriety of sexual expression in marriage was accepted by New Testament writers. Because sexual intercourse is honorable in a proper marriage relationship there need be no hesitancy to express this love and commitment (cf. Heb. 13:4).

Paul recognized the seriousness of sexual compatibility when he cautioned the Corinthians against sexual abstinence in marriage without complete mutual consent, even for a limited time (cf. 1 Cor. 7:5). Such a spiritual purpose as prayer cannot justify the risk of conflict in which one of the partners becomes tempted outside the marriage. Piper understands Paul's passage to demand that "both parties are responsible for each other, to protect each other from physical and mental hurt, through excessive or defective activity of the instinct." [11]

E. G. Selwyn includes sexual compatibility in the meaning of Peter's advice to husbands to "live considerately with your wives, bestowing honor on the woman as the weaker sex" (1 Peter 3:7, RSV). Harriet Mowrer in *Personality Adjustment and Domestic*

Discord agrees that to "live considerately" must include sex needs, and she says "the phase of marriage relations in which conflict first originates is that of sex. This is probably true because it is the earliest relationship demanding an adjustment."

Although the theme of subordination is a dominant one in New Testament husband-wife relationships, it is noticeable that the theme is not applied to the area of sexual relationship. On the other hand, the emphasis in this area is that of meeting the needs of each partner and of consideration for the desires of each other. The concept of "self-control" (*egkrateia*) as a Christian grace serves to equalize the principle of surrender when applied to this area of husband-wife relationship.

No direct application or command for "self-control" in marriage sexual relationships is made in the New Testament. However, as a Christian grace it is appropriate to the expression of consideration which is prescribed. Paul does use *egkrateia* to refer to sexual self-control which is necessary outside of marriage (cf. Cor. 7:9). Later he commends it as a grace expected of the believer in every area of life (cf. 1 Cor. 9:25). The degree of self-control which is necessary outside marriage differs greatly from that within a union. Yet it is reasonable to expect that some self-control will be necessary, the amount varying in the particular circumstances of the marriage.

One of the most basic concepts for preventing and correcting conflicts in this area is for marriage partners to view each other as real persons. The kind of love which has been described previously for marriage is one which will not allow the "using" of another person. A love which has no desire to exploit but only a desire to give one's self prevents sexuality from becoming a problem in marriage. Yet the achievement of such love is not readily accessible to all who enter marriage.

More has been written in recent years on the problems of sexual adjustment than on any other area of marriage. This reflects not only a culture, at least Western, which has become extremely conscious of sexual emancipation but also the basic symbolism of sexual intercourse in marriage. Perhaps too much emphasis has been placed on achieving sexual harmony to the degree of de-emphasizing social, vocational, and religious aspects of marriage. Marital adjustment is not completed in the achievement of successful sexual relationships. The theological considerations expressed above could do much to bring a sense of redemption to human sexuality. All indicators point toward an increasing need of redemption in this area in the coming years.

As we have observed, the areas of conflict discussed here (and all other conflicts) do not necessarily express themselves in one isolated relationship of marriage. In fact, conflict at one point in marriage is only a symptom of a more basic conflict in another area. The task of Christian marriage is to recognize the possibility and cause of conflict and to seek a basis for satisfactory solution. The simple presence of conflicts does not mean a marriage must be dissolved, else no relationship could stand.

The principles enunciated in considering these three areas furnish tools for reshaping other conflictual areas. Money, vocation, personality needs, children, and husband-wife roles are some of the other major adjustments which assault marital bliss if conflict arises. If the committed believer comes to understand the nature and functioning of Christian marriage, he has in hand good defenses against any of these assaults. Yet these must be shared concepts of both partners if they are to be truly effective. Where these principles cannot be effective by the inability, unwillingness, or lack of understanding on the part of one or both partners, divorce is usually the solvent. In the next two chapters we shall consider its propriety, if any exists, in view of Jesus' ethic, redemptive ministry, and teaching.

9. Jesus' Ideal: No Divorce

One of the most controversial and perplexing problems of current society is divorce. It was an equally controversial subject among first-century Jews. Just as the rabbis expressed wide diversity of opinion about it, so there is little unanimous agreement among the theologians today. While nearly all societies recognize divorce as something of a necessity, most of them do so reluctantly.

Jesus' recorded words on the subject have in no sense settled the issue. There is disagreement about the meaning of his words and about their originality. His attitude toward divorce must be seen as an integral part of his whole ethic. It is reasonable to assume that Jesus' treatment of divorce was not different from his consideration of other matters pertaining to the will of God. Therefore, it is necessary to consider first the character of his ethic.

The Absolute Ethic of Jesus

In contrast to the Jewish morality of his day, Jesus thought radically about the problems of sin and of love. This is demonstrated clearly in his comparisons in the Sermon on the Mount (Matt. 5–7). Here he shows how sin goes beyond that which the Law allows, and that love demands more than the Law requires. Therefore, as Rudolph Bultmann has so pointedly stated, "Jesus approaches ethics as radical obedience to the demand of God." [1]

The beginning point of Jesus' ethic is his attitude toward the kingdom of God. H. E. W. Turner states it: "Our Lord's ethical teaching begins not with a certain attitude toward the world but rather with the Kingdom of God." [2] Jesus confronted men with the kingdom and the demand that men surrender themselves to this reign of God. Nothing less than perfect obedience satisfied the demand of God on human life. Thus, out of his basic consideration of the kingdom of God, he arrived at the divine command, "You, therefore, must be perfect, as your heavenly Father is perfect" (Matt. 5:48, RSV).

The ground principle for this perfection is the command to love (cf. Mark 12:28-34). This surpasses every legal demand and in truth becomes "the formulation of an absolute ethic of love." [3] This love is first a total commitment of one's self to God. It is followed by a complete regard for the personhood of others.

Jesus' ethic has been characterized in several ways to describe its uniqueness. William Manson uses the term "existential" to describe this ethic, because it demands the total life commitment for its realization. Its absoluteness is demonstrated in the uncompromising directness with which Jesus presented it. In fact, the ideals of Jesus appear humanly unattainable in their entirety. Jesus intended them to be so, for he realized the radical nature of sin as well as love. His concern was to show the demand of God, not to accommodate his ethic to human ability. Yet he was always concerned with and conscious of human weakness.

Hence, what Jesus presented in his teaching was the ideal of human life in the presence of God. T. W. Manson describes it thus:

In other words, the ideal picture of human life which Jesus draws in what he has to say about morals is a picture of life in the Kingdom of God on earth, life as it may be lived by men who acknowledge one supreme loyalty, in whose hearts one supreme passion burns; and it is only as we hear the call to that loyalty and feel that passion that the moral teaching of Jesus grows luminous.[4]

Having seen the absoluteness of Jesus' ethic, it is time to recognize the context of grace into which he placed his ethic in his ministry. This furnished the connection between his demand for righteousness and the "gospel" of Jesus. He demonstrated not only the demand of God but also his redeeming love. Jesus demonstrated how this redemptive love could turn men toward the absolutes of his ethic. It is this love which calls for a response in which complete surrender is made to the will of God.

Jesus recognized that the human situation existed far below the ideal of divine-human relations. William Manson has pointed out that "we cannot read the Gospels without encountering on every page the evidence that pity for man in the tragic situation wrought by sin was a factor giving shape and content to Jesus' thought of the nature of divine-human relations." [5] Thus the ministry of Jesus was entirely one of redemption.

This fact prevented Jesus from applying his ethic in stereotyped pattern upon every individual and situation. Rather, he confronted each new human situation from the viewpoint of personal redemption. This helps to explain the variety of ways in which Jesus responded to the needs of men.

The most determining factor in Jesus' approach to human problems was the response he met. In each case he demanded that which would involve every area of human relations. The purpose of Jesus' ethic is that the lives of his followers may be ordered in the presence of the kingdom of God which presses upon them.

It then becomes evident that the absolute ethic of Jesus was addressed specifically to his followers, not to society as a whole. George S. Duncan says that "the Christian ethic . . . [is] in the message of Jesus intimately connected with discipleship, and springs spontaneously from a right relation to God who is Father and King." [6] That many of Jesus' sayings were addressed specifically to his disciples and that the distinction is made is shown in the phrase, "It shall not be so among you" (Matt. 20:26).

Thus, when we approach any field of human relations, such as husband-wife relations, it is necessary to keep before us both the absolute ethic of Jesus and the redeeming grace in which he exercised his ministry. Divorce must be considered both from the viewpoint of the absolute will of God *and* the broken situation of humanity. Only God's grace can bridge the gap between these high and separated cliffs.

Jesus' Words Concerning Divorce

Having outlined the framework of Jesus' ethic, it is now possible to see divorce within this larger setting. It is impossible to arrive at a valid estimation of Jesus' position on divorce without first giving minute consideration to the accounts of Jesus' words. These accounts bristle with problems and demand both a consideration of the Synoptic problem and some reference to form criticism. In the following pages we shall attempt to arrive at the hard core of Jesus' words and thought on the subject. Each of the Synoptics differs in many respects from the other two in the accounts on divorce. Here are the accounts as given in the Revised Standard Version:

Mark 10:2–12
And Pharisees came up and in order to test him asked, "Is it lawful for a man to divorce his wife?" He answered them, "What did Moses command you?" They said, "Moses allowed a man to write a certificate of divorce, and to put her away." But Jesus said to them, "For your hardness of heart he wrote you this commandment. But from the beginning of creation, 'God made them male and female.' 'For this reason a man shall leave his father and mother and be joined to his wife, and the two shall become one.' So they are no longer two but one. What therefore God has joined together, let not man put asunder." And in the house the disciples asked him again about this matter. And he said to them, "Whoever divorces his wife and marries another, commits adultery against her; and if she divorces her husband and marries another, she commits adultery.

Luke 16:18
"Every one who divorces his wife and marries another commits adultery, and he who marries a woman divorced from her husband commits adultery."

Matthew 19:3–9
And Pharisees came up to him and tested him by asking, "Is it lawful to divorce one's wife for any cause?" He answered, "Have you not

read that he who made them from the beginning made them male and female, and said, 'For this reason a man shall leave his father and mother and be joined to his wife, and the two shall become one'? So they are no longer two but one. What therefore God has joined together, let no man put asunder." They said to him, "Why then did Moses command one to give a certificate of divorce, and to put her away?" He said to them, "For your hardness of heart Moses allowed you to divorce your wives, but from the beginning it was not so. And I say to you: whoever divorces his wife, except for unchastity, and marries another, commits adultery."

Matthew 5:31–32
"It was also said, "Whoever divorces his wife, let him give her a certificate of divorce.' But I say to you that every one who divorces his wife, except on the ground of unchastity, makes her an adulteress; and whoever marries a divorced woman commits adultery."

It is noticed that in the Markan and Matthaean accounts the teaching of Jesus on divorce is presented as his first teaching beyond Jordan. These two also agree that the teaching is in the context of a test to determine "what is lawful." Various form critics, such as Albertz, Bultmann, Taylor, and Redlish, agree in labeling the account an apothegm or a pronouncement story. This is the kind of account which culminates in a saying which expresses an ethical or religious precept.

From here disagreement, both in the accounts and among interpreters, becomes marked. The question raised in Mark concerns the lawfulness of divorce "at all"; Matthew adds "for any cause." Thus, Matthew makes it a decision in a rabbinic dispute about which are valid reasons for divorce. This raises the question as to the motive on the part of the inquirers in asking the test question. There are numerous answers.

The Matthew account lends itself to the dispute of Hillel and Shammai in which the meaning of the "unseemly thing" of Deuteronomy 24:1 was contested. John A. Broadus doubts that the rabbinic dispute is the background because for Jesus to take a strict view would make him serve immorality.[7] However, both Amram and R. H. Charles prefer the Matthaean account because of the then current controversy.

From Mark's viewpoint, Kirsopp Lake and others have suggested that the motive of the questioning was to endanger Jesus by extracting from him a pronouncement against the divorce of Herod (cf. Mark 6:17 ff.).[8] W. C. Allen gives the most natural and plausible explanation by saying, "The questioners probably knew that Christ taught His disciples that marriage ought to be indissoluble, and they came to get from Him a public statement which would set Him in conflict with the Mosaic Law."[9] In the first century divorce was everywhere accepted so that Jesus must have given a unique teaching about marriage, which gave the Pharisees some hope of trapping him.

Continuing to Mark 10:3-5, it is noticed that these verses are paralleled in Matthew by verses 7 and 8 of chapter 19. Thus, Matthew places Jesus' pronouncement of "one flesh" before the Mosaic discussion. B. H. Streeter prefers Matthew's arrangement, placing the reference to Moses in the Pharisees' mouths and making Jesus' final rejoinder more effective by showing that divorce was a permissive arrangement. However, a study of Matthew shows that he avoided putting questions in the mouth of Jesus, which probably explains the order here. This change of the persons who did the questioning may have been prompted by objection to "command" in Jesus' mouth and "allow" in the Pharisees' mouths. By the change of persons the order of these words is left intact.

The reference to "a certificate of divorce" is taken from the Deuteronomic prescriptions. The phrase "to put her away" of both accounts brings out the meaning of the Septuagint's "and he shall send her out of his house" (Deut. 24:1, LXX). The permissive nature of the Mosaic command is made explicit in Matthew where Jesus uses "allow." It is implicit in Mark by the construction of the phrase in verse 5, "For your hardness of heart he wrote you this commandment." This is to show that the nature and purpose of the Mosaic law was a concession in the presence of sin in order to curb sin.

The original purpose of the divorce bill was to protect the wife.

In most ancient societies she could be sent away at the whim of
the husband. It was this kind of "hardness of heart" which made
divorce necessary in ancient Hebrew society. H. B. Swete explains "hardness of heart" as follows:

The word must be taken to mean a condition of insensibility to the
call of God, and not only want of consideration for a fellow creature
which the present context suggests, but incapacity for comprehending
this Divine love, implying the absence of an unselfish love for men, and
both result from the withering up of the moral nature under the power
of a practical unbelief.[10]

The use of the word in the Septuagint renders it "uncircum-
cision of heart, rage, or pride, of the heart, crooked and stub-
born." In other words, divorce was first conceived as an
accommodation in human society to curb sin and perverseness.

Mark 10:6–9 and Parallels

Note that Matthew repeats the argument from creation at the
end of verse 8, applying it negatively to the Mosaic legislation.
This he could do because in Matthew Jesus begins with the creation account and refers to God as "he who made." Common in all
the accounts, the male and female creation reference is taken
from Genesis 1:27, which Jesus links with Genesis 2:24, in stating
the purpose, arrangement, and nature of marriage. Matthew does
use the fuller quotation from Genesis 2:24, with the phrase "and
be joined to his wife." The culminating statement of the passage
is, "What therefore God has joined together, let not man put
asunder" (RSV). Here the indissolubility of marriage is emphatically stated. If this is God's ideal for marriage, what place does
divorce have?

The term *choridzeto* is taken by Vincent Taylor to be a
technical term for divorce.[11] However, neither here nor in
1 Corinthians 7:10 is the thought concerned with divorce as an
institution but rather as the rending asunder of a sacred union.

The point of verse 9 is that man (*anthropos*) has no prerogative to dissolve what God has united. Marriage is a creation of God. The desire to limit these pronouncements to ideally happy marriages is an interpretation of convenience.

Mark 10:10–12 and Parallels

This section, which in Mark is a private discourse with Jesus' disciples, is the most controversial passage on marriage in the New Testament. The other three forms of the saying are found in Matthew 5:32; 19:9; and Luke 16:18. In addition, Paul refers to the Lord's pronouncement in 1 Corinthians 7:10–11.

The first phrase of all four accounts concerns the action of a man's divorcing his wife with the result that the man commits adultery in so doing. Matthew (19:9) drops the thought here but Mark explains "against her." Mark's account would certainly not be acceptable to Jewish Matthew, since adultery was conceived in Jewish law as intercourse between a married woman and a man other than her husband. However, this does not destroy the originality of the Markan phrase, since obviously Jesus intended to give an entirely new meaning to "commit adultery." It is understandable that he would broaden its meaning to include injury done to the wife.

Luke also omits the "against her" and uses another form which is the simple active "he commits adultery." In Matthew's other account (5:32) the phrase "he makes her to become an adulteress" appears. Of these variations, T. W. Manson accepts Luke as the original form from Q and explains the rest as follows:

Mark 10:11a gives the sense of Luke 16:18a and makes it more precise by the addition of the words "against her." Mark 10:12 is a misunderstanding of the *Aramaic* Luke 16:18b. Matthew 19:9 is Mark 10:11 modified in the direction of the Shammaite legal doctrine by the addition of the excepting clause. Matthew 5:32 is an expanded version of the part of the dictum represented by Luke 16:18b. It may be the M version of the saying. It contains the excepting clause, which here *may* belong to the original text of M.[12]

The other possibility is that both Mark and Q contained the saying and Matthew was influenced in both directions, as demonstrated in the two forms in which it appears.

Jesus' new meaning to the term "adultery" concerned the
violation of the marriage bond without specifically referring to a
case of postnuptial fornication. This meaning of adultery consists
of repudiating the marriage bond and regarding one's self as un-
committed to a "one-flesh" union. All of the accounts, except
Matthew 19:9, show this attitude by the hypothetical remarriage
of the person who violates the first union.

E. Lyttelton has given an excellent presentation of the force
of Jesus' words in the following passage:

> The word for "to put away" does not mean simply to send out of
> the house to live apart, but to divorce formally under the impression
> (false) that the first contract is thereby wholly dissolved.
> The husband who thus lightly thinks to dissolve the marriage
> contract by divorcing his wife is not said simply to commit adultery,
> but to "make her commit adultery."
> The woman is not said to *become* an adulteress voluntarily but
> deliberately, to be *made* one: so that the expression would cover the
> case of a wife who has done nothing but fail to retain her husband's
> love, and then has been quite unwillingly "put away." It is as if the
> mere fact of her existence, apart from any wrong thought she may
> have harbored in her mind, is an offense against the divine law; she is
> made in her person to embody the revolt of society against the purity
> and completeness of the marriage union.
> They have construed it as though the cumbrous formalities of the
> *get* obliterated wholly the Sacred bond which preceded it: and when
> a husband wantonly and in obedience to his own whim declares before
> the whole world that his life partner is wholly sundered from him and
> is free for remarriage, he declares a lie, and she, however much in her
> heart may dissent from this, is made in virtue of her false position to
> share in the communities' disloyalty to God's decree.[13]

Thus, adultery may be committed in three ways: (1) by a
person who divorces his partner in quest of freedom when there
is no reason for him to be released; (2) by a third person who

marries a divorcee; (3) by the person who is divorced, even against her own will.

The Exception Clauses

One of the large problems of the verses considered here is the authenticity of Matthew's exception clauses in 5:32 and 19:9. Various attempts have been made to substantiate the clauses, especially by Catholic theologians who *a priori* accept Matthew as the First Gospel.

Bruce Vawter discusses a number of these explanations and then defends the "preteritive" interpretation which goes back to Augustine.[14] This interpretation does not allow divorce in case of fornication; rather, the exception clauses (on linguistic grounds) are looked upon as saying that Jesus was not even considering the case of fornication. In this case the phrase would be translated, "setting aside the matter of fornication," or, "fornication is not involved." If thus allowed, Jesus raised as large a problem as he answered by leaving the case of fornication entirely undefined and, on the basis of this interpretation, without reason, since the next explanation is unacceptable to the "preteritive."

R. H. Charles also accepts Matthew as the original account and, on historical ground, shows that Jesus was not able to consider the case of fornication since conviction for this was followed by death.[15] Therefore, Jesus made the exception in deference to the Mosaic law of adultery (cf. Deut. 22:22), and Matthew has correctly recorded Jesus' position. Mark, he feels, omitted the phrase because his Gentile readers would not understand. By accepting Jewish law, Jesus has implicitly then allowed divorce and remarriage on this ground.

Another explanation by Bayard H. Jones accepts the Matthew clauses with the explanation that they refer to premarital unchastity, since the death penalty was prescribed for marital unfaithfulness.[16] It is doubtful that if the death penalty had been in effect, Jesus would have accommodated his teaching to Mosaic law. He certainly did not hesitate to show that the law was a concession on account of sin which ran contrary to the actual purposes of God.

The first doubts about the clauses were raised in modern scholarship by Holtzmann and Wellhausen who were soon joined by more conservative B. Weiss and Salmon. As Synoptic criticism developed and the sources were isolated, Lake and others found the origin of the sources in the need for legislation in the church. The three facts of Synoptic study which affect the problem are: (1) Mark was used by the other two Synoptists, especially Matthew; (2) the First Gospel had another source which was used in common with Luke (especially Luke 9:51 to 18:24); (3) Matthew made many minor changes in the material received from these sources.

From the standpoint of chronology, then, the Matthaean account is later. Added to this is the fact that Luke also omits the clauses so that the two earlier accounts (Mark and Luke) give no record of their existence. Nor does Paul show any acquaintance with such a concession when he states the words of Christ which he received in 1 Corinthians 7:10–11. A survey of patristic writers by J. P. Arendzen shows that there is no evidence before Nicea that these clauses were interpreted to authorize breaking of the marriage bond so that the partners could be free to remarry.[17]

Another important factor rendering suspect the exception clauses is the impossibility of reconciling the concession, which pays deference to Mosaic law, with the absolute ethic of Jesus discussed above. He has, indeed, gone no further than the school of Shammai if the clauses are his accommodation. Hence, both historical criticism and ethical consistency militate against the clauses as part of Jesus' original pronouncement. However, as will be demonstrated below, these words may represent the mind of Christ ethically applied to a less-than-ideal situation.

The originality of Mark 10:12 is also partly contested, but mostly by those who prefer Matthew's account. For example,

Basil Redlich goes so far as to assign all that is beyond verse 9 to the early church as a concession to the Roman readers and a reflection of the views of the church itself. The main ground of objection is that Jewish law provided no opportunity for women to divorce their husbands; thus, Jesus would not be discussing such a possibility. Vincent Taylor accepts the reading of Beza and the Old Latin texts to avoid having Jesus comment on the action of women. C. C. Torrey achieves the same effect by using Aramaic to show that the participle should be passive. Some who accept the verse as entirely original find in the divorce of Herodias an example to which Jesus may refer. Stronger support for the verse is found in the fact, however, that Paul reports Jesus as having addressed part of his saying to women (cf. 1 Cor. 7:10). In fact, Kirsopp Lake, observing Paul's statement of woman-man order, is ready to accept the codices which reverse the order of verses 11 and 12.

In Mark 10:2 the original question was placed in good Jewish form, but it is only in the pronouncement of Jesus in verse 12 that the woman is given consideration. In light of Jesus' higher authority than Moses' law, the universal advocation of his ethic, and the increasing Gentile influence which he must have met, it is not surprising that he made application of the indissolubility of marriage to both sexes. However, the account which is least objectionable is that of Luke 16:18, where the participle describing the divorced woman is passive. Thus, with Manson, we conclude that the Q form (cf. Luke 16:18) is the more original.

Summary

During the course of examining the accounts of Jesus' words, we have discussed much of his thought on divorce. Yet, it remains to bring this thought into clearer focus. His stand on divorce can only be seen if viewed from his position with regard to marriage in general. This sequence is different from that of our own age, when often marriage is seen from the standpoint of divorce.

The main lines of Jesus' thought on marriage have been drawn in earlier chapters. However, two or three stand out in regard to divorce. Man was created male and female so that marriage would be a fundamental human relationship. So marriage is a part of God's good creation. Therefore, the dissolution of a marriage is the destruction of a creation which God ordained.

To a woman who asked what God had been doing since his completion of creation, Rabbi José replied, "He has been engaged in bringing about marriages." This principle does not suggest that every existing marriage has been arranged by God; rather; it simply recognizes that in every marriage, those who enter enter a relation made possible by the creation of God. In this sense they are responsible to God for what they make of it. It is in this sense that the sin of divorce exists—a relationship which was intended to be sacred becomes exploited or destroyed.

Another aspect of Jesus' view of marriage which must be considered when divorce is discussed is that marriage is a complete and indissoluble union. Marriage establishes a permanent human relationship which must be entered into with full commitment to its mutual responsibilities. This absolute view of marriage countenances no thought of divorce. Thus, both in its origin and nature, Christian marriage in its ideal sense finds no place for dissolution by human will.

The most revolutionary conclusion Jesus drew on divorce came from seeing marriage in its basic structure as a relationship. Viewing marriage thus, he saw divorce as adultery in a new and broadened sense. *Moicheuein* was used by Jesus to mean a violation of the marriage bond for any reason; it is not just an example of postnuptial unchastity ordinarily designated by *porneia*. Since the classic meaning of adultery is an act of unfaithfulness or an injury to the marriage relationship, Jesus saw divorce as the irreparable destruction of the union. Hence, divorce of any kind is, in that sense, adultery.

Although the offense of divorce as injury to the woman as well as to the man was novel in Jesus' teaching, it had been implicit in Hebrew thought. In this respect Jesus invoked an equality in marriage by recognizing the injury done to the woman and to the relationship. Whether Mark 10:12 is accepted as original or not, its point is conveyed in Jesus' teaching; and, when the time came that a woman could institute divorce, her action, too, would be adultery.

It is obvious from the manner in which Jesus expresses his view on divorce that he is not so concerned with the formality of a written document as he is with that which it symbolized—a ruptured relationship. Marriage, in his view, was not a legal or institutional contract; rather, it was a sacred relationship which was not to be violated under any condition. Here the relational character of his teaching is especially prominent.

We have emphasized the ideal and absolute view of Jesus with regard to God's intention for marriage. However, there is implicit in his teaching the recognition of human imperfection and sin. He pointed out that divorce was originally made necessary by the presence of human sin and the inability to realize the marriage relationship in its intention.

Conditions other than ideal must be considered in the light of God's will for those circumstances. The early church discovered it necessary to apply both the redeeming ministry of Jesus as well as his absolute ethic to such situations. Divorce is always less than the ideal, but human life is of the same nature.

10. The Reality:
Some Broken Marriages

In the preceding chapter we have seen how clearly Jesus stated his absolute ethic with regard to marriage. Divorce is not the revealed will of God for believers who desire his will. Yet, it is impossible to ignore Jesus' recognition of the needs of sinful humanity as he exercised his redemptive ministry. Few of Jesus' interpreters have seen as completely as did he the depths of man's brokenness. If his absolute ethic served to accentuate that brokenness, his redemptive ministry revealed his complete understanding in sympathy with man in it.

When the early church was confronted with this brokenness, an absolute ethic could not be enforced. Some attempt must be made to apply it though, since to early Christians the words of Jesus were law. It is out of these concrete situations where the absolute ethic is fitted to conditions of an imperfect world that the possibility of a redemptive ministry was made available. There is evidence that at least two such occasions were confronted in the New Testament. These we shall consider here to see the direction of the applications made.

Paul and Divorce

Doubtless others had faced the problem of a possible divorce, but Paul was the first to write about it whose letters we have. It was one of the many domestic and ecclesiastical problems in the church at Corinth. We have already touched on the reply given in 1 Corinthians 7:10-12, but here we may again envisage the situation and follow the principles of his solution.

106

There were in the Corinthian church converts whose husbands or wives had remained unbelievers. The words of Jesus had been received in the church and Christians knew that divorce was not God's intention. Yet, some of the unbelieving partners were threatening separation from their believing partners. This was leaving the believers with a sense of responsibility to maintain the marriage at all costs. It may even be that some believers doubted that they should stay with their unbelieving partners. In these cases it seems that religious incompatibility was the chief problem.

Paul begins with the principle of indissolubility, which is retained even when the marriage is one of believer with unbeliever. Especially should the believer attempt to keep the "one-flesh" union intact, considering neither separation if a woman nor divorce if a man. The apostle was certainly committed to the conclusion that divorce was not the solution to religious conflict. He even refers, in Romans 7:2–3, to divorce as an adulterous rupture, albeit in a different context from this. Believers who can manage a peaceful married life with an unbeliever have no need of divorce. A spiritual life is not an escape from marital responsibilities or personal conflicts.

Yet in these circumstances the believer may have no choice in the matter. What shall be done if the unbeliever demands or desires a separation? Paul here appealed to a principle that takes over when the principle of indissolubility fails. It is the principle of peace. He saw peace as one of the chief characteristics of the Christian life. For example, he says, "So much as lieth in you, live peaceably with all men." Certainly Jesus expected that peace would characterize the lives of his disciples (cf. Matt. 5:9). Thus, if the unbeliever desires to be free to the extent of destroying the relationship of peace, separation is better than constant warfare. The believer will be injured in the destruction of the marriage but not guilty for its dissolution.

In verse 11, Paul encourages the Christian partner always to hold out the possibility of reconciliation. The guiding principle for this possibility, as well as the prospect of a permanent dissolution, is that of seeking a redemptive way out of a less-than-ideal situation. For the committed person there is always the possibility of seeking the will of God in situations, which if not ideal, are nevertheless real.

Hence in this passage, while Paul acknowledges that he has no word of Christ for this particular occasion (cf. v. 12), he makes what he believes to be the application consistent with the over-all teaching of Christ. Robertson and Plummer say, "He applies Christ's ruling as far as it will reach in the case of a mixed union." [1] Yet, the significant recognition for our present discussion is that here the first missionary-theologian found divorce a necessary possibility in an imperfect world where the absolute ethic of Jesus would not be accepted by some marriage partners. Acknowledgment of this fact does not open the way for promiscuous divorce nor does it destroy the teaching of Jesus on marriage; rather, it is the redemptive approach to a real situation where the "hardness of heart" still is present. We turn now to consider another such occasion more clearly connected to Jesus himself.

The Application in Matthew

The exception clauses of Matthew 5:32, "except on the ground of unchastity," and 19:9, "except for unchastity," are highly significant for the divorce question. Even if Jesus did not originally include them in his statement (as we have discussed earlier), they have a contribution to make.

Three possible sources for the clauses can be suggested: (1) Jesus may have made such a private application of his ideal on another occasion; (2) the disciples may have been forced to such an application in the early church; or (3) this may be the attempt of Matthew to report Christ as a new Moses, or lawgiver, and he did this in deference to the Jewish law.

The most conclusive decision which can be made on the basis of available evidence is that the application was made by some early moral theologian who had the words and mind of Christ.[2]

L. H. Marshall finds it necessary to reject the clause entirely when he says:

So the "saving clause" twice introduced into St. Matthew's Gospel is to be dismissed as a later addition to the text, occasioned by the difficulty of carrying out in practice the uncompromising teaching of Jesus. It is to the ideal course that Jesus summoned men, and what He urged was that they should never think of terms of divorce at all. In a prophetic, and not a legalistic, spirit He is calling on men to consider not how they can most easily cancel their marriage vows, but rather how they can make marriage the indissoluble thing that God intended it to be.[3]

Following the earlier assumption about the clauses, the early church or a theologian was confronted with an occasion of fornication and was pressed to give a decision. In view of the high ethical ideal of Christ on marriage some practical application was needed. Since early Christians viewed the words of Jesus as law, an enactment of his words was sought in this case.

Dibelius observes about the clauses: "This very form of the saying shows that Jesus' words were already being used for legal ordering of daily life, and that the proclamation of the coming kingdom was being made over into a catechism for continued existence in the old world." [4]

Since Jesus had conceded that in Mosaic legislation divorce was conceived to recognize such a violation, it was natural to revert to Mosaic prescription when marriage was so destroyed. Fornication in Jewish eyes defiled a woman so that she was no longer acceptable to live with her husband, for injury had thereby been done to the husband.

Considering the deep and profound meaning of sex in marriage, it is symbolic of a ruptured relationship when extramarital relationships are experienced by either man or wife. Hence, the very logical conclusion found in Matthew that if such an experience so destroys the relationship that it cannot be restored divorce is the acknowledgment of such a destruction.

However, divorce was not commanded, and within the ethic

of Jesus there was provided the means whereby even marital infidelity need not destroy the marriage relationship. Jesus had taught that a right relationship of man to God can only be established through the experience of forgiveness and that this forgiveness must be extended by the believer (cf. Matt. 6:14–15). If the marriage partners are committed to God and there is a repentant attitude on the part of the offender, the offended can forgive and even fornication need not lead to divorce. In this way, the principle of forgiveness aided by love can sustain the principle of indissolubility.

Here, then, is a very early application of the redemptive approach to the marriage relationship where, in this case, fornication had destroyed it. Obviously, from the controversies of the schools of Hillel and Shammai, as well as later Christian interpretations, legal interpretations of such clauses can lead to divorce on almost any grounds. For example, Augustine wrote:

> Since the Lord permits that a wife be put away on account of fornication, another question arises as to how the word "fornication" is to be understood in this context; whether it is to be taken in the sense in which everybody understands it, or in the sense in which the Scriptures usually employ it. In the first case, it would be understood to denote the kind of fornication that is committed in unchaste acts; in the other case, as we have already noted, it would be understood as denoting every sinful corruption—such as idolatry or avarice—and, consequently every transgression of the Law through sinful desire.[5]

It thus becomes immediately evident that legal interpretation is not the answer. It is important only to recognize that very early the Christian community had to deal with the problem of a destroyed relationship.

Applications of the Patristic Writers

The majority of the patristic writers, including Hermas, Justin Martyr, Tertullian, Theophilus, Clement of Alexandria, and Origen, accept the exception clauses and permit divorce in case of fornication but limit divorce to this one condition. Acceptance of this one condition alone reflects the interpretive practice of the Fathers to treat Christ's words as law rather than as ethical ideals. Origen is the exception, however. He pleads for a broader application when he says:

It might be a subject of inquiry if on this account He hinders anyone from putting away a wife, unless she be caught in fornication, for any other reason, as for example for poisoning, or for the destruction during the absence of the husband from the home of an infant born to them, or any other form of murder whatever.[6]

This plea for a more consistent approach to divorce was short-lived and eventually divorce was prohibited entirely. Thus the church removed itself from the brokenness of the human situation and invited circumvention to meet a legal enactment. Hermas saw that fornication need not destroy the marriage, provided the adulterer was repentant. No consideration was given to Paul's case of believers married to unbelievers. Patristic interpretation solidified the process of legalizing the New Testament teaching on marriage and divorce. In this view marriage lost its relational character and became a formal contract to be preserved at all costs. The Fathers lost sight of the relationship they were fighting to protect.

Here then are the earliest examples of attempts to meet the human situation with an absolute ethic. An imperfect world will not allow the universal application of such an ethic. The recognition of this fact does not invite the discarding of Jesus' ethic; rather, it points up the very need for such divine idealism. Human life not only needs the challenge of an absolute standard but in the striving for this standard there is the opportunity for redemptive grace to be effective. At few points have biblical interpreters been more blind than when dealing with divorce in the light of this absolute ethic.

It is basic to recognize that Jesus was not primarily concerned with marriage as an institution but as a relationship of life through which the will of God could be realized. Nor was he concerned with his absolute ethic as a standard to be legally administered; rather, through this ethic was to be discovered the will of God in human relationships. Divorce is not God's intention in marriage, but neither is divorce the unpardonable sin to which God's redemptive grace cannot extend. Divorce was conceived for a world where men exist in imperfect and often broken relationships. To absolutize marriage against divorce is to ignore the relational character of marriage.

It is necessary to find the will of God even in the imperfect relationships of life. Some of these relationships are imperfect through wills other than those of the believers involved. Some are imperfect because the persons involved are incapable of living in good relationships. The will of God cannot be considered abstractly apart from the conditions of one's life. Hence, as long as imperfection and "hardness of heart" remain, divorce will be a last resort necessity for some people.

When the need for considering divorce arises in a marriage relationship it is always a symptom of inner problems experienced by one or both of the marriage partners. Thus, it becomes necessary for those concerned to seek what is most redemptive for their lives if they are committed to God. What Jesus made unmistakably clear in his discussion of marriage and divorce was that divorce is to be considered only when all other possibilities of reconciliation and restoration proved ineffective.

The principle of indissolubility can never be ignored. Divorce becomes a necessity only when the relationship has been irreparably destroyed, not when it has only been injured. For the believer, if ever divorce is approached, it must be with a view to redemption and healing for those involved.

The alternative to recognizing the reality of marriage disintegration by divorce is the maintenance of a facade in many cases. This is true even where one or both of the marriage partners are believers. Divorce, in the sense of a destroyed relationship, is as much a reality when it is psychological as when it is legal. Two people who live together in silent coexistence may be meeting the legal requirements for the principle of indissolubility but they have already destroyed the intention of it. When all communication between two people has broken down, divorce has already taken effect.

Inability to "live in peace" may express itself in open warfare or in cold isolation of two individuals in the same house. Surely this is no less a "living in sin" than legal divorce, as divorce is sometimes looked upon by those who so interpret it. The refusal to acknowledge the reality of human brokenness in marriage then excludes also the possibility of a redemptive ministry of Christ in marriage. Of course, even in cases of psychological divorce there should always be held up the prospect of reconciliation, but "hardness of heart" is still with us.

Out of the applications Jesus' first followers made of his ethic, there have been noted certain principles which can aid in a decision about divorce. Mace recognizes one of these in contrast to legal enforcement:

The law is concerned with offense and retribution, with the neatly balanced justice that makes the punishment fit the crime. In grave matters this principle may be necessary to keep the peace. But so long as marriage remains in any sense a relationship, it must be conducted upon an entirely different principle—the principle of repentance and forgiveness.[7]

The experiences of forgiveness and redeeming love can restore a relationship where the one who has injured it has repented. On the other hand, we have seen above that the principle of peace and sanctification sometimes leaves no alternative but to recognize that a relationship has been hopelessly injured or ruptured. In the New Testament, divorce has always been a last resort tragedy; yet, even the first Christians found it sometimes necessary.

11. Remarriage?

The corollary to divorce is remarriage. The large majority of those who experience divorce will sooner or later face this question too. Those whose marriage is terminated by death may also need guidance at this point. Ethically there is a vast difference between these two groups, but in the United States, at least, there are other differences as well. These are pointed out by Jessie Bernard in her study titled *Remarriage*.

The question of remarriage evokes problems for both minister and layman. Should the minister officiate at weddings of those who are remarrying after divorce? If so, on what basis?

Some ministers refuse to marry any divorced person. This may raise the question that if it is wrong for the minister to perform weddings for divorced persons, should such persons be allowed in the fellowship of the church?

Some ministers try to follow strictly "legal scriptural grounds" by officiating only at marriages of the "innocent party," on the basis of the exception clauses. This raises the problem of the minister's establishing who is the "innocent" one, since almost without exception those who request marriage after divorce will profess to be the "innocent." Then, usually those few who do admit any responsibility for the failure of the former marriage do so on some other basis than that allowed in the exception clauses. In fact, while the minister is considering for whom he will perform marriages, he also may want to consider whether to perform marriages for believer with nonbeliever—a condition which is clearly prohibited by Paul.

114

Many active Christians find themselves faced with the consequences of a divorce and seek earnestly the will of God for the rest of their lives. Some of these will have become believers after they have experienced divorce but find conditions in which no reconciliation is possible. Others will want to consider remarriage after the death of a partner, but with some hesitancy for fear of appearing disloyal or actually feeling betrayal to the deceased.

Easy answers to such questions do not appear to the serious student of the New Testament. For these problems, as in many others which have arisen in these pages, the New Testament does not provide neat, ready-to-wear answers. New Testament writers, as well as Jesus, answered problems only as they faced them, and even then only in a culture of a particular age. However, there are some answers given, some theological bases, and some implications of thought which should be looked for even in the problem of remarriage. The New Testament continues to speak!

Remarriage After Divorce

The problem of remarriage after divorce is one of the most vexing problems of life, bearing wide disagreement when appeal is made to the Scriptures. Of special import in the history of the question has been the use of the exceptive clauses of Matthew, which makes remarriage permissible for the innocent party where the divorce has been on the grounds of adultery.

R. H. Charles is one who, in agreement with the Eastern Church, finds evidence in these clauses that the innocent party is free to remarry.[1] McNeile, who assigns the clauses to a later time in origin, feels that remarriage is implied and says that "whether the writer of the gloss thought that the divorcee was free in such a case to marry again is not clear, though it seems to be implied." [2] E. Lyttleton goes a step further and says that the clauses "imply that divorce consequent on conjugal infidelity is the human pronouncement of a dissolution already effected, which leaves *both parties* free to marry again." [3] However, this is an argument from silence, since obviously the concern of the passage is divorce.

Matthew says in 5:32*b* that whoever marries the woman innocently divorced commits adultery. The most that can be said for the Matthaean account is that if the exceptions are extended to the remarriage, as well as divorce, they do not *prohibit* remarriage in the case of fornication. However, the intent of the exception clauses relates far more to the question of divorce than to remarriage, although in Matthew 19:9, the exception clause makes remarriage seem permissible. Here again, the exception clauses seem to obscure the absolute teaching of Jesus.

When this is realized none of the Synoptic accounts, unless Matthew 19:9 is treated as a legal loophole, gives the *right* to remarry. In fact, Mark (10:11–12) and Luke (16:18) include re-marriage in the flat assertion that it is adultery.[4] McNeile says that "the re-marriage of either party can claim the authority neither of Jesus nor the Church." [5] We arrive again then at the realization of Jesus' absolute ethic.

This absolute prohibition of remarriage stems from the absolute prohibition of divorce, or the principle of indissolubility in which adultery is the breaking of the marital relationship. Jesus was primarily concerned with the preservation of the marriage bond which he emphasized in the words, "What therefore, God has joined, man is not to separate" (cf. Mark 10:9).

Lyttleton explains that "the meaning of adultery is simply such ignoring of the bond as a man is guilty of who . . . regards himself as unconnected with her by any contract." [6] The adultery of a second marriage would be involved in the fact that the first bond is indissoluble in the sense it can never be as though it had not been. Thus, remarriage becomes the second symbol (divorce is the first) of a destroyed marriage relationship and the seal that it will not be repaired.

Paul also exhibits his devotion to the principle of indissolubility when considering remarriage. However, R. H. Charles finds grounds for remarriage in Paul's words of 1 Corinthians 7:10–12,15. He rejects Paul's parenthetic statement in verse 11 ("but if she be separated, she is to remain unmarried or be reconciled to her husband") and goes on to show that Paul gave the unbelieving partner who is deserted by an unbelieving partner the liberty to remarry. This is done by identifying *ou dedoulotai* of verse 15 with *eleuthera* of verse 39 and saying, "This fact suggests that the right of remarriage is here conceded to the believing husband or wife." [7]

The first half of verse 11 may not be the words of Christ as received by Paul (as Charles says), but it certainly is a parenthetic statement *by Paul*, even if it sounds as though it is "not addressed to Jews." [8] It reflects that Paul was not encouraging remarriages and was concerned, as was his Master, that the marriage relationship be repaired if possible.

That Paul's attitude toward divorce and remarriage was identical with Christ's is evident from the assumption he makes in Romans 7:3: "Accordingly, she will be called an adulteress if she lives with another man while her husband is alive. But if her husband dies she is free from that law, and if she marries another man she is not an adulteress" (RSV). Here he specifically states without qualification that remarriage is adultery.

Considering this concept of marriage and divorce as an ideal, in Paul's release of the believing partner in the case of wilful desertion by an unbeliever, it is open to doubtful question that he meant to allow remarriage by *ou dedoulotai*.

Another important consideration for remarriage in Paul's theology is his pronounced eschatology, as seen in 1 Corinthians 7. In view of the impending *eschaton* which shades this chapter, it is doubtful that he would have advised the Corinthians to remarry. This would also prevent his making any applications of a redemptive nature to the problem of remarriage for the believers. However, we shall examine the matter later to determine if he provided any basis for such applications.

Among the Ante-Nicene Fathers, remarriage was not understood to be allowed by the exception clauses. As observed above, the clauses were accepted by them as genuine. However, both Arendzen[9] and Howington[10] have shown, all the Fathers refuse the divorced person (for whatever cause) remarriage. Augustine later was very emphatic about a husband or wife's remaining unmarried or seeking reconciliation on the basis of repentance of the guilty in cases of fornication.[11] The expressed attitude was that since marriage was indissoluble, even though a couple separated, they remained bound in wedlock.

From all available evidence, we conclude that Jesus did not entertain remarriage in his teaching. Because there was no place for divorce in the absolute ethic, no opportunity for remarriage was offered. Remarriage was mentioned only in a negative way as a usual accompaniment of divorce but it is never advised. In the New Testament the writers were not called upon to consider remarriage by itself, except as John the Baptist denounced Herod Antipas for his adulterous second marriage (cf. Mark 6:18). Thus, it can be established that neither Jesus nor Paul granted any *right* for second marriages, whether to the "innocent" or to the "guilty." The ethic of Jesus, as well as that of his first interpreters, viewed the first marriage as a one-flesh creation of God, indissoluble in nature. Thus remarriage has no place in this ideal.

Having considered then the ideal of Jesus' absolute ethic, there remains to be considered the implications of his redemptive ministry toward remarriage in the same manner that we have seen them already in divorce. In the early church the exception clauses and Paul's believer-unbeliever advice are demonstrations of the adaptation of the no divorce absolute to concrete, imperfect situations. Except by association with divorce in the exception clauses we have no like examples with remarriage, but the same principles are present.

If the character of all the rest of Jesus' ministry can be applied to the problem of remarriage then the ultimate question is, "What is most redemptive for the lives of the persons involved?" This kind of question is obviously open to rationalization, but it is the question which Jesus constantly demonstrated in his ministry toward people of broken and imperfect predicament.

If remarriages are ever contracted, in view of the above, it must be only when the first relationship has been so completely destroyed that there is no possibility of restitution. A second consideration must be the moral and spiritual advancement of those involved, since the sanctification of the total person is the will of God (cf. 1 Thess. 4:2). Here it may be that under less eschatological conditions Paul would have offered the same advice on some remarriages that he offered on marriage, "for it is better to marry than to burn" (1 Cor. 7:9).

Very careful attention must be given to the question of whether one who has had a marital relationship destroyed would be capable of building into a second relationship that which was lacking in the first. When attention is called to the relational character of the marriage bond with its physical, mental, and spiritual aspects, it becomes apparent that decisions about second marriages cannot be made on a "guilty" and "innocent" basis. It takes little more than superficial observation to note that while one partner may be overtly guilty of marital destruction, the other partner could be covertly more responsible.

It behooves every person who experiences marital dissolution to inquire as to his own need of help and redemption, regardless of the overt aspects of the situation. Quotations of Scripture verses obviously cannot provide a one-flesh union, nor can they eliminate the necessity of making such decisions as remarriage out of the whole context of life, seeking redemption and sanctification. Only in consideration of the true nature and sanctity of marriage and the spiritual life of the individuals involved is it possible to arrive at the will of God for those committed to him in a less-than-ideal condition.

Remarriage After the Death of a Partner

In our discussion on the earthly constitution of marriage the foundation was laid for consideration of the problem of remarriage after death. Directly, Jesus did not discuss the problem. The only inferences which can be drawn from him are in his words found in the question of the Sadducees in Mark 12:18–27. Here Jesus does not dispute but tacitly accepts the idea of remarriage in levirate marriage. Thus, although it is not the main point of the discussion, yet coupled with Jesus' pronouncement upon the lack of marriage in the heavenly realm, it provides a valid basis for a widow or a widower considering remarriage. If marriage is a relationship of earthly existence, the attachments of which are severed by death, then such remarriage cannot be objected to on theological grounds.

Paul also makes some pronouncements which are more directly relevant and which have been referred to earlier. As an analogy of freedom from the Law, the apostle shows that a woman is bound to her husband only so long as he lives, and after death she commits no sin by marrying another (cf. Rom. 7:1–3). He repeats this principle in 1 Corinthians 7:39 and grants that a widow may remarry at her will. However, in the last part of the verse he makes the qualification that she marry a fellow believer "in the Lord." The hesitancy he expresses is part of his reluctance for believers who have not married to enter marriage at all. This is in view of the expected *parousia* which will render all earthly relationships unimportant.

In the Pastorals a situation regarding young widows is confronted. These were probably supported by the church as fulfilling a particular office but some had changed their minds about the unmarried state and wanted to marry (cf. 1 Tim. 5:11–12). This was considered a denial of their vows and a refusal of the service of Christ.

Some of these widows were causing further problems by becoming talebearers in their idle time and destroying the ministry of the church (cf. v. 13). As a remedy for the problem, the younger women were advised to return to marriage and serve Christ through a well-ordered and godly home. Later, reference will be made to those who may not have ever been married but who belonged to the order anyway. As is shown in 1 Timothy 5:3, the concern here is for "real widows."

The main point for our present discussion is that here in the early church young widows were allowed and advised to remarry.

Turning to the post-New Testament church fathers, however, the picture changes. They did not exhibit an understanding of marriage as being an earthly existence, nor were they willing to allow those whose partners had died to remarry. Athenagoras (A.D. 177) says, "He who deprives himself of his first wife, even though she be dead, is a cloaked adulterer, resisting the hand of God." [12]

Tertullian emphatically states that "if those whom God hath conjoined man shall not separate by divorce, it is equally congruous that those whom God has separated by death man is not to conjoin by marriage." [13]

So sacred and intimate a relation as marriage could convey the impression that death does not dissolve the bond, but the New Testament concept, in recognizing that its constitution is earthly, does not betray either the sacredness nor the intimacy of the marriage relationship.

Although the advice given in the New Testament on remarriage after death of a partner is consonant with the nature of marriage, some of the same considerations must be given to remarriage here as noted after divorce. Marriage is always a sacred relationship and there are peculiar difficulties to be faced in every second marriage, varying with the circumstances. Even a healthy one-flesh relationship in a first marriage does not guarantee a second such experience. In fact, the dangers of projecting former patterns and experiences into the new relationship are great. Paul's advice that it be "only in the Lord" must apply as much to the individual's own spiritual life as to the marriage partner's being committed to God.

Before summing up the considerations for remarriage we pause to note an interesting experiment in the life of the early church which provided an alternative to remarriage.

An Alternative to Remarriage

By establishing the office of widow the early church attempted to meet the needs of this group and utilize the lives of these Christian women. Very little is recorded in the New Testament concerning the office but enough to show its importance and perhaps its roots. Almost from the beginning the Christian church was faced with the care of widows and the first "deacons" were appointed to the matter (cf. Acts 6:1 ff.). It can be conjectured that the problem increased as the church attempted to care for those who no longer had husbands to provide for them, and out of this they were given duties that they might render special service in the church.

A rather extended discussion of the office of widow is given in 1 Timothy 5:3–16. Qualifications for the office included establishing that the candidate was an actual widow (cf. v. 3), since it seems that some were enrolled who were not. The minimum age for enrolment was sixty and only those who had been married once or were not polygamists could qualify (v. 9). Her reputation had to be one of faithful and humble service in the church, demonstrating her desire to do menial service (cf. v. 10). There seems also to have been required that those enrolled not have families to care for them, suggesting that they were supported by the church (cf. vv. 4, 6).

A vow to this office was made, which seems to have been intended for the remainder of their lives (cf. v. 12). The duties included spending time in prayer for the church's ministry and the needs of the people, service to the sick, caring for visitors, and aiding in the church's ministry (cf. vv. 5, 10). The group apparently became sizeable, making it difficult to provide sufficient service to keep them occupied and sufficient funds for their provisions (cf. vv. 13, 16).

The Ante-Nicene writings take cognizance of the office of widow, which continued to have the same problems of young widows remarrying, in sufficient support, and lack of fulfilment of their duties. Another peculiar problem that plagued the church was enrolment of not only young women but some who had never been married at all. Tertullian says,

> I know plainly, that in a certain place a virgin of less than twenty years of age has been placed in the order of *widows*! Whereas if the bishop had been bound to accord her any relief, he might, of course, have done it in some other way without detriment to the respect due to discipline; that such a miracle, not to say monster, should not be pointed at in the church, a *virgin widow*! [14]

Young widows' remarrying is referred to in the third-century document *Didascalia Apostolorum* which says, "Appoint as a widow one that is not under fifty years old, who in some sort, by reason of her years, shall be remote from the suspicion of taking a second husband." [15]

Thus did the early church attempt to provide occupation and support for those whom death had separated. It had to be recognized that second marriages were almost as natural as first ones, but the early church had difficulty accepting it. It is worthy of note that the intent of the early church was to provide creative and redemptive avenues for these persons.

Even though the office fell into abuse and later disuse, it is in the spirit of its Master whenever the fellowship of the church seeks earnestly to meet the needs of persons in distress. The failure of this experiment points up also the need for serious and creative thought to be given the question of remarriage in a wholesome, Christian atmosphere.

In summation, we arrive at the conclusion that remarriage for the divorced must be faced on the same plane as divorce itself. The absolute ethic of Jesus alone, in its ideal for marriage, would exclude any divorce or remarriage (as well as continuous incompatible marriages). Every believer committed to God should be committed to this principle of indissolubility. Yet Jesus was keenly aware that his absolute ethic was being cast into a world of imperfection, sin, and hardness of heart. Unless we would absolutize only one area of life (marriage) it is necessary to follow the redemptive example of Jesus as well as recognize his ideal.

The redemptive approach to life demands that the question of remarriage at least be left open to those who find themselves yet in human brokenness. Jesus nowhere made divorce or remarriage the unpardonable sin, though admittedly either is less than his intention. It is not only conceivable but probable that the most redemptive course for some who have divorced is remarriage, e.g., a Christian mother with children to rear whose lives will be further maimed without the presence of a loving father. Certainly grave caution and unselfish prayer would need to accompany such a decision. Recent contributions of personal and marriage counseling furnish greater possibilities for finding the redemptive way in remarriage.

Again, although the early church allowed it hesitatingly, there is nothing in the biblical constitution of marriage to prevent remarriage after death of a partner. The alternative of the office of widow persisted for some time but never provided an entirely satisfactory solution.

One who has been committed to a life of marriage finds difficulty adjusting to a celibate life. We have seen earlier that a celibate life is a gift, and this is realized perhaps most clearly by those who have been married and return to single life by death or divorce. Yet, while many must face the question of remarriage, others find both happiness and creative possibility of life without re-entering marriage. Whether considering a first marriage or remarriage, the committed believer will feel the imperative of: "Let all men take care, that this covenant shall ever remain sacred."

12. Celibacy

In the name of Christianity marriage often has been disparaged or at best looked upon as a second-rate condition for Christian living. Where celibacy has been exalted it has usually been on the basis of a dualism which tends to view a physical contact as somewhat inherently evil.

The fact that Jesus did not marry is often pointed out. It is the attempt of this chapter to consider Jesus' actual attitude toward celibacy and marriage and behind that to discover the bases for his attitudes.

Jesus' View of Physical Life

A consideration of Jesus' view of earthly life inevitably must confront eschatology. A detailed discussion is not possible here, but the main lines serve as guides for evaluation of earthly relationships.

The problem of celibacy at present runs in at least two directions. First, there is the problem of celibacy for those who may feel voluntarily called to a life of celibacy in order to fulfil some other vocation. Second, the problem confronts many people in our society because of the numerical majority of women over men. There are several millions for whom no statistical marriage partner is available. Added to this is the fact of earlier death of men than women, leaving many who will live out the rest of their lives in involuntary celibacy.

Is celibacy, on any ground, superior to marriage? Or, is mar-

125

riage a necessity for a life of fulfilment and purpose? From the
New Testament we look for answers to these life situations.

Jesus proclaimed that the kingdom had "drawn near" and
repentance was the only preparation for it (cf. Matt. 4:17; 10:7;
Luke 10:9–11). He also said the kingdom had actually come
and was present in the midst of the people by the power of
exorcism and forgiveness of sin which he himself exercised (cf.
Luke 17:21; 11:20; Matt. 12:28).

Still in another strain of preaching Jesus looked to the ap-
proaching *eschaton* and the Son of man "with power" (Mark
8:38; 13:26; Matt. 10:23; Luke 22:16,18). The coming *eschaton*
and the destruction of Jerusalem are intertwined in the Little
Apocalypse (Mark 13) to the extent that it is difficult to determine the proximity of the *eschaton* in the mind of Jesus.

There is no absolute standard by which to judge the influence
of the early church and its experience upon the record. Valid
evidence does point to the fact that the *eschaton* was in the mind
of Jesus, and he expected a consummation of the in-breaking
kingdom. In fact, it appeared so luminously in his mind that its
precise or even approximate date meant nothing. The facts of its
coming and its propensity demanded immediate and complete
preparation.

The coming *eschaton* profoundly affected Jesus' attitude toward
human relationships and physical life, for in the context of the
eschatological event, these things receded in importance. Childbearing, marriage, and family relationships will be disrupted as
tribulations preceding the event begin to transpire (cf. Mark
13:17; Matt. 24:27; Mark 13:12).

Jesus did not show any abhorrence of marriage and family relationships; they were simply minimized by the gigantic cloud of
eschatological hope and the coming kingdom. This cloud is allowed to recede when Jesus is asked to discuss marriage, divorce,
and the will of God about relationships of life, so that his asceticism is apocalyptic if it exists at all. By this expectancy, however,
Jesus was able to show that nothing must take precedence over

man's relationship to God, not even marriage (cf. Luke 14:20).

Thus, Jesus' attitude toward material things and earthly relationships was determined by his more basic attitude toward the kingdom of God. This, to Jesus, was life's greatest good; preparation for this in-breaking kingdom obscures all other concerns (cf. Luke 12:22–31). Any of life's relationships may need to be renounced or foregone if preparation for the kingdom demands it in a particular situation (cf. Luke 14:26 f.).

Renunciation as an end in itself finds no place in Jesus' teaching and is never considered meritorious as such. The ethic of Jesus, to be sure, is one of sacrifice, but always sacrifice for a purpose. As Goguel says, "He demanded sacrifices for Himself, or the Gospel, or for the sake of the Kingdom." [1] His demands upon individuals were not uniform; rather, they were made in light of one's spiritual needs. For example, the rich young ruler was asked to sell all he had, while the demands upon Zacchaeus were confined to fourfold restitution.

Jesus did not claim to be an ascetic; rather, contrasting himself with John the Baptist (cf. Luke 7:33–34), he demonstrated respect for the normal duties and relationships of life insofar as they did not conflict with the higher duty to God (cf. Mark 8:13). His own sacrifices and renunciations were made by virtue of his sense of vocation to the task of redemption.

Jesus himself was a celibate; his disciples were not (cf. Mark 1:30–31; 1 Cor. 9:5). His only demand for celibacy was made in favor of a higher surrender to the kingdom of God, where marriage and service would be in conflict. Jesus certainly respected the marriage relationship, as we have seen in the above one-flesh discussion. His one direct statement on celibacy must be considered in light of that discussion and his entire ethic.

The disciples said to him, "If such is the case of a man with his wife, it is not expedient to marry." But he said to them, "Not all men can receive this precept, but only those to whom it is given. For there are eunuchs who have been so from birth, and there are eunuchs who have been made eunuchs by men, and there are eunuchs who have made themselves eunuchs for the sake of the kingdom of heaven. He who is able to receive this, let him receive it" (Matt. 19:10–12, RSV).

There is general agreement among scholars that this saying was not necessarily in this context when originally spoken. The affinity of subjects is the suggested basis for its inclusion in this section. Also, both sayings begin with the same Greek word (*aitia*—cause, basis, or reason). The interest here centers in the saying of Jesus, which he qualifies by stating that "this saying" is not a general rule, because he realizes that not all can "find room for" or "be capable of containing" it. It is expressly directed to those "for whom it is given."

Because of these verses, Calvin looked upon continence as "a special gift bestowed upon very few, and only those who have been appointed by God can endure the sacrifices of the celibate life." [2] No intimation is given here that this applies to a sacerdotal order. The fact that celibacy is in this sense a gift would abrogate any human claim to virtue for its possession.

Jesus gives three instances of "to whom it is given" or three cases where celibacy may be expected. The first two are established by unalterable circumstances. The third is certainly metaphorical in the sense that abstinence, not mutilation, is intended. Otto Piper describes the three classes thus:

(1) Some persons have been made incapable of sex life, having been castrated or sterilized. (2) In other cases, there are persons who are unsuited by nature for sex life, either because they do not possess the physical ability or because they are not capable—or capable only in a small degree—of sex excitement. (3) The third group consists of those who have silenced the voice of sex within themselves because they believe that they must dispense with marriage for the sake of their work on behalf of the Kingdom of God. [3]

Certainly the last case alone is voluntary exercise of the gift. The final admonition is more explicit in its emphasis of the gift nature than it sounds. Literally, he says "the one capable of making room (for this) is to make room." It may be paraphrased: "If you have the gift, exercise it."

A comparison of Paul's view of eschatology with that of Jesus shows agreement in the main lines; yet some differences of language and emphases appear. Less "realized" eschatology is apparent with Paul, and that which is presented is in the sense of being "in Christ" in the Old Aeon (cf. Eph. 1:21; Gal. 1:14; 2 Cor. 4:4). The Old Aeon overlaps with the New Aeon, resulting in the believers' living in two worlds simultaneously. Apocalyptic hope appears brighter on the horizon with the apostle than with his Master. God's present demand, as Paul saw it, was not in terms of the pressing kingdom but rather because of the "in Christ" position of the believer. The time is short, however, until Christ will return and total realization of salvation will be obtained (cf. Eph. 1:14).

One of the elements in Paul's eschatology was that the time is short (cf. 1 Cor. 7:29); but before the appearing of Christ, the man of lawlessness will appear (cf. 2 Thess. 2). The distance in the future of these two events seems to move in both directions, perhaps depending upon Paul's own circumstances and political conditions, as he viewed them.

Paul further believed that when Christ appears there will be a resurrection of the righteous and those alive will meet Christ (cf. 1 Cor. 15:51 ff.; 1 Thess. 4:14). At this time Christ will be exalted to the throne of dominion over all powers and will receive glory from the whole world in recognition of his position (cf. Eph. 1:21 ff.; Phil. 2:9–11). With this *eschaton* will come the destruction of all earthly relationships, and the full realization of salvation will obscure every other concern, especially distinctions of sex and race (cf. Gal. 3:28; 1 Cor. 9:29–31).

This "time is short" attitude greatly affected the ethic of Paul. In fact, Joseph Fletcher thinks Paul advised a race suicide on this basis.[4] Paul did not contend that such relationships as marriage were unimportant; rather, in view of tribulations soon to begin when these relationships would be destroyed, it was useless to enter them unless necessary.

It is notable that apart from his eschatological expectation, there was no abhorrence of earthly relationships, as appeared in the Corinthian church. Paul claimed his own rights to both wife and material support in such a way as to reveal a normal Jewish attitude toward these needs as a part of human life created by God (cf. 1 Cor. 9:5; 2 Thess. 3:9). Piper has understood Paul when he says, "Like his master he developed his ideas of sex on the basis of an eschatological view of life as a whole, a fact which gave a dialectical character to these ideas as to all his doctrines." [5]

Basically, Paul's ethics were derived from his "in Christ" theology, which elevated an "according to the spirit" kind of existence as opposed to an "according to the flesh" kind of existence (cf. Rom. 8:1–15).[6] This antithesis was not a dualism in the sense of deprecating physical existence; rather, it was an orientation of the person toward spiritual values with an acceptance of the physical as a means to sanctification (cf. Col. 3:1–3).

While this understanding of Paul's ethical basis is helpful, it does not entirely dissolve the difficulty of fixing Paul's position on such questions as marriage and celibacy. He dealt with these matters in their concrete, specific instances. Nor is it easy to know the exact nature of the problem dealt with; hence the difficulty of evaluating his answers, such as in 1 Corinthians 7, which we now consider.

1 Corinthians 7

Both the problem and the manner of Paul's apologetic are to be considered before the answers can be assured. In this chapter the undercoating of an extreme asceticism in the Corinthian church shows through. Paul, although himself committed to a celibate life, combats this extreme. The problem is first hinted in

verse 2, where Paul is arguing for marriage, even if on the low
plane as a preventive function from immorality.

Within marriage Paul finds it necessary to urge a sexual compatibility (cf. vv. 3–5), discouraging marital abstinence. He dis-
courages divorce or separation where one partner is an unbeliever
and encourages the believer to live a life of peace (cf. vv. 10 ff.).
In fact, he emphasizes that the Christian should remain in the
same relationship in which he was called into grace (cf. vv. 17 ff.).
Paul has to assure those who are contemplating entering marriage
that no sin is thus committed (cf. v. 36). The tone of these
admonitions echoes a tender overcoming of a complete disdain for
the marriage relationship, both actual and contemplated. Enslin
states the problem: "Doubt had risen in the minds of some as to
the propriety of Christians marrying at all or even of continuing
living in the married state." [7]

A little different in nature, but not otherwise unknown, is the
indirect method of Paul's polemic in this chapter. He begins on
the side of his opposition and moves from there to a corrected
position. Chadwick notices this same method of polemic in 1
Corinthians 6, where Paul deals with a libertinism by admitting
in the beginning the "fundamental position that the Christian is
free from all restraint." [8] He used this same method (almost in
ridicule) in accepting the self-appointed position of the Corinthians (cf. 1 Cor. 4:8–12). It is the method of accepting some of
the premises while rejecting others, or rejecting false conclusions
drawn. This apostolic opportunism will be pointed out in the
exegesis of the chapter which we now consider.

Now concerning the matters about which you wrote. It is well for a
man not to touch a woman. But because of the temptation to
immorality, each man should have his own wife and each woman her
own husband. The husband should give to his wife her conjugal rights,
and likewise the wife to her husband. For the wife does not rule over
her own body, but the husband does; likewise the husband does not
rule over his own body, but the wife does. Do not refuse one another

except perhaps by agreement for a season, that you may devote yourselves to prayer; but then come together again, lest Satan tempt you through lack of self-control. I say this by way of concession, not of command. I wish that all were as I myself am. But each has his own special gift from God, one of one kind and one of another (7:1–7, RSV).

The "matters" referred to involved the extreme asceticism asserted by the Corinthian inquirers. The admission, "It is well for a man not to touch a woman" is directed to an unmarried man (*anthropos*), not to a husband (*aner*). This statement was likely the position of the Corinthians, as they asserted absolutely that Christians should not be married. "Well" (*kalos*) is used here to describe the quality of this assertion; it is not a comparison with another mode of action. It is the assertion of being able to have liberty and Paul later shows he was not intending to abolish marriage. The attitude is commendable but not commanded.

The adversative "but" introduces another consideration to the acceptability of the celibate ideal. With reference to the low estimate of marriage which Paul seems to take here, Robertson and Plummer point out: "The apostle is not discussing the characteristics of the ideal married life; he is answering questions put to him by Christians who had to live in such a city as Corinth." [9] The case for monogamy is implied in this verse. Not only is marriage a human necessity but in the very nature of marriage a debt is created between partners that is sexual (cf. v. 3). Otherwise, how would marriage prevent *porneia*? There is no disparagement here of the sexual aspect of marriage.

The principle of marriage relationship, which Paul states in verse 4, is a logical outgrowth of the head-body unity understood from Ephesians (cf. 5:21–33). Equal duties are placed upon marriage partners in the mutual surrender of their bodies for the expression of sexual love. This principle is quite unexpected in a milieu of male superiority and must be accounted for in part by Christian influence. The "authority" granted here demands an atmosphere of *agape* for its proper exercise.

This is demonstrated in verse 5, in the admonition to preserve sexual compatibility. Complete agreement is called for in sexual relations, including even abstinence for spiritual development. The Koine text, which adds "fasting," is interesting in that it connects the surrender of food with sexual abstinence, here presented as a form of fasting for the purpose of prayers. Caution is expressed even in this noble practice, lest prolonged abstinence should deteriorate the preventive function of marriage. Hodge enumerates the conditions of this abstinence: "With mutual consent, for a limited time, for the purpose of special devotion, and with the definite intention of reunion." [10]

It is generally agreed that "this" of verse 6 refers to the whole of verses 2–5. "Concession" is too strong in this verse. His point is that since he did not have a direct command from the Lord on this problem he is giving his advice. He finds it necessary to fall back on this personal advice in verses 25 and 40 also. He is not commanding marriage but he wants his readers to realize the practical necessity of it and its normal relations.

Against the preceding section it can only be understood that Paul was at this time celibate, whether he had ever been married or not. He recognizes both the celibate and the married state but emphasizes that the *charisma* of the person should determine the choice. Nor does Paul attach any intrinsic merit here to either state. Thus by showing the practical necessity and inherent obligations of marriage, Paul has discouraged the ascetic extremists while yet embracing a celibate life for himself.

In the next section we read:

To the unmarried and the widows I say that it is well for them to remain single as I do. But if they cannot exercise self-control, they should marry. For it is better to marry than to be aflame with passion. To the married I give charge, not I but the Lord, that the wife should not separate from her husband (but if she does, let her remain single or else be reconciled to her husband)—and that the husband should not divorce his wife. To the rest I say, not the Lord, that if any brother has a wife who is an unbeliever, and she consents to live with him, he should not divorce her. If any woman has a husband who is an unbeliever, and he consents to live with her, she should not divorce him. For the unbelieving husband is consecrated through his wife, and the unbelieving wife is consecrated through her husband. Otherwise, your children would be unclean, but as it is they are holy. But if the unbelieving partner desires to separate, let it be so; in such a case the brother or sister is not bound. For God has called us to peace. Wife, how do you know whether you will save your husband? Husband, how do you know whether you will save your wife? (7:8–16).

As Paul turns here to advise various groups, his celibate position and his approval of it become apparent. Those addressed include those who have not been married and those whose marriage death has ended (widows). Notice that both here and in verses 39–40, widows are the only side considered, not widowers since men were much freer.

The use of "well" (*kalos*) in verse 8 is probably a little stronger than in verse 1, though there is still no comparative degree intimated. On the basis of what has been stated in the previous section, Paul is here considering those who do possess the gift of continence. Also, in verse 9 he makes clear that celibacy is not for those without the gift; marriage is the preferred state for them. His appeal is to practical reason, not divine command; but in it he recognizes marriage as a satisfactory solution to human passion. The New Testament concept of sexual morality makes no allowance for its exercise outside marriage.

Paul's command in verse 10 is based on Christ's teaching on divorce. The intent of this verse is grasped by Hodge who says, "The plain doctrine of the passage before us . . . is that marriage is an indissoluble covenant between one man and one woman for life, admitting neither of polygamy or divorce." [11] Here Paul attacks the evident tendency of married Corinthians to separate. From the tone of verse 12, the preceding words are addressed to believing people.

Beginning with verse 12, the apostle attempts to deal with a situation to which Jesus had not addressed himself; i.e., the case of a marriage between a believer and an unbeliever. If mutual consent to live together peacefully exists, there is no reason for a believing husband or wife to seek separation or divorce. Paul shows great respect for the preservation of the marriage relationship in thus applying his understanding of Jesus' teaching to the case.

Sacramentarian commentators have argued for baptismal connection as the explanation of verse 14. However, in the absence of any baptismal reference here and the presence of the Hebrew concept of holy people, it is more probable that Paul drew on this background. For the Corinthians it gave a reason for the validity of a mixed marriage. Hodge refers to this: "The Hebrew people were sanctified. . . . All who joined them, or who were intimately connected with them, became in the same sense, holy. Their children were holy; so were their wives." [12] Paul does not mean that salvation comes by connection of marriage relationship but rather that the marriage relationship is valid and that children born are not therefore illegitimate.

Turning to a different situation, the ethic of believers does not apply to unbelievers. If the unbeliever takes the initiative in the separation, no obligation is placed upon the believer. The New Testament ideal of husband-wife relationships is applicable primarily to believers and cannot be legislated for all society.

R. H. Charles connects the "is not bound" of verse 15 with "she is free" of verse 39, and concludes that Paul is giving permission for remarriage here.[13] It is doubtful that Paul has remarriage in mind, but it may be permissible under the conditions. The principle behind Paul's willingness for separation is that of a life of peace into which the believer is called. When he considers the motive of witness in remaining together, he casts doubt upon the effectiveness of such witness under these unhappy conditions (v. 16). Peter is hopeful of such witness; however, he is not considering the case of an unwilling partner (cf. 1 Peter 3:1–2).

Paul takes a mediating course in the Corinthian marriage extremes and his argument therefore bears an oscillating character.

However, his position is based on a concept of individual calling in which each must discover and pursue his own calling. This, as a general principle, is the content of Paul's digression in verses 17 through 24:

> Only, let every one lead the life which the Lord has assigned to him, and in which God has called him. This is my rule in all the churches. Was any one at the time of his call already circumcised? Let him not seek to remove the marks of circumcision. Was any one at the time of his call uncircumcised? Let him not seek circumcision. For neither circumcision counts for anything nor uncircumcision, but keeping the commandments of God. Every one should remain in the state in which he was called. Were you a slave when called? Never mind. But if you can gain your freedom, avail yourself of the opportunity. For he who was called in the Lord as a slave is a freedman of the Lord. Likewise he who was free when called is a slave of Christ. You were bought with a price; do not become slaves of men. So, brethren, in whatever state each was called, there let him remain with God.

It is a life of peace to which the individual is called in Christ, accepting whatever limitations this may imply. The instances referred to are but illustrations of the principle.

In the rest of the chapter (vv. 25–40), Paul elaborates on the problems of marrying and the advisability of it.

> Now concerning the unmarried, I have no command of the Lord, but I give my opinion as one who by the Lord's mercy is trustworthy. I think that in view of the impending distress it is well for a person to remain as he is. Are you bound to a wife? Do not seek to be free. Are you free from a wife? Do not seek marriage. But if you marry, you do not sin, and if a girl marries she does not sin. Yet those who marry will have worldly troubles, and I would spare you that. I mean, brethren, the appointed time has grown very short; from now on, let those who have wives live as though they had none, and those who mourn as though they were not mourning, and those who rejoice as though they were not rejoicing, and those who buy as though they had no goods, and those who deal with the world as though they had no dealings with it. For the form of this world is passing away. I want you to be free from anxieties. The unmarried man is anxious about the affairs of the Lord, how to please the Lord; but the married man is

anxious about worldly affairs, how to please his wife, and his interests are divided. And the unmarried woman or girl is anxious about the affairs of the Lord, how to be holy in body and spirit; but the married woman is anxious about worldly affairs, how to please her husband. I say this for your own benefit, not to lay any restraint upon you, but to promote good order and to secure your undivided devotion to the Lord. If any one thinks that he is not behaving properly toward his betrothed, if his passions are strong, and it has to be, let him do as he wishes; let them marry—it is no sin. But whoever is firmly established in his heart, being under no necessity but having his desire under control, and has determined this in his heart, to keep her as his betrothed, he will do well. So that he who marries his betrothed does well; and he who refrains from marriage will do better. A wife is bound to her husband as long as he lives. If the husband dies, she is free to be married to whom she wishes, only in the Lord. But in my judgment she is happier if she remains as she is. And I think that I have the Spirit of God.

He confesses that he had no saying of Jesus to which he could refer. What he gives is his own opinion, but he feels that as a recipient of God's grace he is qualified to make these pronouncements.

The apostle gives in verses 26–28 the reason for his seeming negative attitude toward marriage. It is "the impending distressing circumstances" which makes him fear for those who would embark. He pleads for neither marriage nor celibacy but to remain in the present state.

The eschatological cloud is rolling in on his judgment. However, even in view of the coming cataclysm, it is not a sin to marry; it is only (in Paul's judgment) unwise. The "tribulation" is recollective of that spoken of by Jesus (cf. Luke 21:23).

This eschatological climax moves closer in Paul's mind, as in verses 29–31 he calls for a renunciation of every earthly interest in the last hour. Earthly relationships will soon be destroyed in the passing of this worldly scheme (cf. 1 John 2:15–17). Following this realization, the apostle in verses 32–35 sets forth the practical advantage of the unmarried state.

Interpreters have made a battleground of verses 36–38 by

disagreeing over the persons addressed. Roman Catholic scholars have resolutely maintained that the passage was addressed to fathers who were considering their daughters.[14] Others have claimed it is a reference to a celibate group known as *virgines subintroductae*. In view of the preceding reference to the *parthenoi* in verse 25, and the subsequent context, the simplest and most apparent reference is to those who have not yet married and yet have tried to restrain themselves because of the extreme ascetic element in the Corinthian church.

The advice to marry is conditional upon the enigmatic *uperakmos*. Since "his virgin" identified the subject "one" as masculine and there is no evident change of subject in the phrase, "if his passions be strong," the subject and predicate adjective should be accepted as masculine and refer to the man. This agrees also in the contrast of the next verse where a condition of complete control is conceived. Under such conditions of necessity, Paul allows marriage but by the next condition he shows a preference for restraint. "Well" is here used of marriage but he uses the comparative "better" to refer to celibacy. Paul's preference is again stated but he is careful not to disparage marriage.

To the widows Paul addresses himself in verse 39. The earthly nature of the marriage relationship is evident by the freedom granted to the widow to remarry; the only restriction placed is that the marriage partner must be a believer (cf. 2 Cor. 6:14). Again the apostle admits freedom but shows a preference for the unmarried state. He seems to know that marriage is right and to be allowed but cannot bring himself to accept it unreservedly. The closing statement shows he does not take his position without some reservation.

Insights into the early church's attitude toward celibacy and marriage are scattered throughout the New Testament. For example, marriage was accepted and expected for those who became bishops and deacons in the church (cf. 1 Tim. 3:2,12). Some writers found it necessary to denounce the depreciation of marriage and to avoid ascetic extremes. In 1 Timothy 4:3–4, an ascetic assertion is refuted as being the teaching of liars "who forbid marriage and enjoin abstinence from foods which God created to be received with thanksgiving by those who believe and know the truth. For everything created by God is good, and nothing is to be rejected if it is received with thanksgiving" (RSV).

Foods and marriage are upheld as good because God has created them. Ascetic extremes, noticed in Corinth, had continued and grown to the proportion that marriage was being completely forbidden. The pastoral Epistles defend marriage, as does the writer of Hebrews in 13:4: "Let marriage be held in honor among all, and let the marriage bed be undefiled; for God will judge the immoral and adulterous." There is a question here whether the statement is declarative or hortatory, but close examination gives favor to hortatory intent. No room is made in this statement for a secondary attitude toward marriage or an exaltation of celibacy.

This review of the various attitudes toward marriage and celibacy represented in the New Testament has not presented an altogether consistent picture. However, there are some main lines of agreement. First, celibacy is recognized as a particular calling and for those who possess the gift of continency and receive such call there is the opportunity for special service for the kingdom of God. Celibacy is not presented as intrinsically meritorious nor even as a higher, more spiritual way of life than marriage. Its merit is in its purpose alone. On the other hand, marriage is viewed as a divinely created arrangement for human life. Its duties and functions are not to be despised. An eschatological cloud alone darkens the future for marriage but this is not always present with New Testament writers.

It should be obvious that neither marriage nor celibacy is the only answer. By the very fact of male and female creation, God has intended human beings to be capable of living in married relationship. However, it follows no more logically that this ability *must* be exercised by all human beings than to conclude that because married couples can have children that they therefore should have as many as possible. Both Jesus and Paul demonstrated a life of fulfilment and purpose apart from marriage. Yet, neither of them assumed that in and of itself celibacy was a mark of superiority.

Thus, for those who may find that voluntarily or involuntarily theirs will be a life of celibacy, life need be neither meaningless nor empty. Just as childless couples will find other ways to make their lives creative, so also will the single person who commits his life to God and finds a Christian calling in his particular state. This commitment leaves open the possibility of either continued celibacy or marriage.

Epilogue

Whole new dimensions of life and Christian ministry are discovered in Jesus' relational view of life. In fact, Christian love is not truly seen until its relational character is recognized. In the progress of this present study, this fact has become increasingly plain. Christian marriage cannot exist on any plane other than the relational level.

By seeing both the divine absolutes and the imperfect human status, we have become aware of the tension in which the Christian lives between these two. These perfect relationship ideals with which Jesus presented marriage are relevant to the human situation. That they are rarely attained is undeniable. However, they serve the very important function of giving direction and providing goals.

The marriage relationship, like all other areas of human existence, is marked by partiality and imperfection when it is viewed in its actual state. While Jesus was presenting his absolutes, he was being confronted constantly with people whose lives were already broken and for whom these ideals were no longer possible. His redemptive ministry became the bridge between these two regions. In his grace he provided the nexus between what is and what ought to be.

Therefore, Christian marriage can be viewed as a valid and vital part of the "upward calling in Christ Jesus." Fortunately, the Christian community to which the gospel was given had time to face some of the practical problems of human life in marriage while those who best knew the mind of Christ were still on the

scene. Too long many of the passages which refer to these problems have been quietly ignored by ministers and churches. Perhaps one of the reasons for this neglect has been the necessity of
distinguishing between the underlying principles and the applications made. The New Testament offers much safe guidance to
Christian marriage but this guidance is not always recognized
at a glance.

It remains for Christians who take seriously not only their
marriage vows but also their commitment to God to discover the
creative possibilities of marriage. We have been confronted re-
peatedly with the fact that the New Testament teachings on
marriage were addressed specifically to the Christian community
and are normative for believers. In fact, it is the Christian commitment which furnishes the dynamic for these creative possibilities. In the orbit of Christian grace marriage is a continually
unfolding relationship. Each shared experience provides the
potential for the enrichment of the relationship through the dis-
covery of new facets in the lives of Christian partners. Whereas
human personality is not static, the wellspring of deeper understanding and mutual appreciation can flow as long as life lasts.
Each "stage" of life offers the possibility of new applications of the
marital concept of one flesh. The meaning of this term is not fully
uncanvassed as long as life is shared.

The creative aspect of human life can be seen nowhere more
clearly than in marriage. The marriage relationship is creative
in two obvious directions. First, the mutually shared life is creative
for human personality. This is true not only of finding personal
fulfilment but also of the evoking of new attitudes and otherwise
unknown potentials of life. Second, the possibilities of procreation
and their subsequent privileges are, indeed, creative. God's
greatest gift bestowed on the Christian *agape* of a believing
husband and wife is that this love should produce another life.
With a Christian view of life, here is one of the high points of
entering into creative activity with God. The creative possibility
of the family is one of God's highest callings to human beings.

In a very real sense, we have seen that Christian marriage after the one-flesh order is the creation of a new self out of two otherwise distinct beings. Thus, husbands and wives may function as complementary parts of that "self." Each has his own role and must consider the needs of the other part of the "self," whether it be the head or the body. To draw the figure further, it may even be suggested that this "self" finds its immortality in its procreation. Only Christian love which finds its motive in the cross experience of Christ for his church is normative for Christian marriage as the head "loves the body." Such is the way of a Christian man with his wife.

This work, which has focused its attention on the relational character of Christian love and drawn from theological concepts for its ideals, suggests further areas of concern in biblical studies. For one thing, a parallel study of the theological basis for parent-child relationships is warranted. There is something to be learned both about our relationship to God as his children and about the ideals of family life as these are drawn from theological understandings. Another possibility has become increasingly prominent through these pages. There is need for relating the biblical material dealt with more closely to the insights of recent psychological studies. No attempt has been made to do this in this work in order that full attention could be given to interpreting the New Testament materials in their historical context.

The mine is not yet exhausted, but the treasures we have been privileged to handle fascinate the imagination. The Christian community has these ideals by which to inspire its participants to live their lives in the married state. The experience of the members will not come up to the absolute ethic of Jesus but husbands and wives who live in the consciousness of his grace will make this and nothing less their goal. It is uniquely to committed believers that the New Testament possibility of becoming "one flesh" is offered.

Notes

Chapter 1

1. H. Wheeler Robinson, "Hebrew Psychology," *The People and the Book*, ed. Arthur S. Peake (Oxford: Clarendon Press, 1957), p. 362.

2. *Ibid.*, p. 14.

3. Aubrey R. Johnson, *The Vitality of the Individual in the Thought of Ancient Israel* (Cardiff: University of Wales Press, 1949), p. 23.

4. J. A. T. Robinson, *The Body: A Study in Pauline Theology* (Chicago: Henry Regnery Co., 1952), p. 16.

5. Otto Piper, *The Christian Interpretation of Sex* (New York: Charles Scribner's Sons, 1941), p. 42.

Chapter 2

1. Seward Hiltner, "Sex, Sin or Salvation?" *Pastoral Psychology*, III (September, 1952), 27.

2. Piper, *op. cit.*, pp. 8-10.

3. *Ibid.*, p. 30.

4. Paul Haupt, "To Know—To Have Sexual Commerce," *Journal of Biblical Literature*, XXXIV (1914), 71-76.

5. Piper, *op. cit.*, p. 54.

6. Reuel Howe, *The Creative Years* (Greenwich, Conn.: Seabury Press, 1959), p. 98.

7. D. S. Bailey, *The Mystery of Love and Marriage* (New York: Harper & Bros., 1952), p. 66.

8. Sylvanus Duvall, "Sex Morals in the Contest of Religion," *Pastoral Psychology*, III (May, 1952), 36.

9. Seward Hiltner, *Sex Ethics and the Kinsey Report* (New York: Association Press, 1953), p. 31.

10. Piper, *op. cit.*, p. 100.

11. E. C. Messenger, *Two in One Flesh* (London: Sands & Co., Ltd., 1950), I, 48.

12. *Ibid.*, II, 174.

Chapter 3

1. Joseph Pedersen, *Israel: Its Life and Culture* (London: Oxford University Press, 1926, 1940), I, 62-63.

2. Alexander Gross (trans.), Saint Chrysostom's "Homilies to the Ephesians," *A Select Library of the Nicene and Post-Nicene Fathers,* ed. Philip Schaff (Grand Rapids: Wm. B. Erdmans, 1956), XX, 144.

3. Francis W. Beare, "The Epistle to the Ephesians: Exegesis," *The Interpreter's Bible,* ed. George Arthur Buttrick (New York: Abingdon Press, 1953), X, 724.

4. Anders Nygren, *Agape and Eros,* trans. Philip S. Watson (Philadelphia: The Westminster Press, rev. 1953), pp. 170 ff.

5. Ezra P. Gould, *A Critical and Exegetical Commentary on the Gospel According to St. Mark*, "The International Critical Commentary" (Edinburgh: T & T Clark, n.d.), p. 229.

6. William G. Cole, *Sex in Christianity and Psychoanalysis* (New York: Oxford University Press, 1955), p. 20.

Chapter 4

1. Thomas Aquinas, *Summa Theologica* (New York: Benziger Brothers, 1917-27), III (Suppl.), q. 65, Art. 1, Cf. also q. 41, Art. 1.

2. Cf. Bailey, *op. cit.*, p. 107.

3. Piper, *op. cit.*, p. 47.

4. Emil Heinrich Brunner, *The Divine Imperative*, trans. Olive Wyon (Philadelphia: The Westminster Press, 1949), pp. 331 f.

5. Messenger, *op. cit.*, III, 50.

6. Thomas Aquinas, *op. cit.*, q. 41, Arts. 3 and 4.

7. Bailey, *op. cit.*, pp. 107 f.

8. David R. Mace, *Whom God Hath Joined* (Philadelphia: The Westminster Press, 1953), p. 71.

9. Pedersen, *op. cit.*, p. 48.

10. E. D. Selwyn, *The First Epistle of St. Peter* (London: The Macmillan Co., Ltd., 1955), pp. 432 ff.

11. Gibson Winter, *Love and Conflict* (Garden City, New York: Doubleday & Co., Inc., 1958), pp. 15 ff.

Chapter 5

1. B. W. Bacon, "The Apostolic Decree Against Acts," *The Expositor,* Ser. 8, VII (1914), 40-61.

2. D. W. Amram, "Adultery," *The Jewish Encyclopedia*, ed. Isidore Singer (12 vols.; New York: Funk & Wagnalls Co., 1946), I, 216.

3. D. S. Bailey, *Homosexuality and the Western Christian Tradition* (London: Longmans, Green, & Co., 1955), p. 8.

4. M. S. Enslin, *The Ethics of Paul* (New York: Harper & Bros., 1930), p. 148.

5. Plato, *Symposium*, trans. W. R. M. Lamb (The Loeb Classical Library), V, 146 f.

6. Piper, *op. cit.*, p. 119.

7. *Ibid.*, pp. 135-36.

Chapter 6

1. John Calvin, *Commentary on the Epistles of Paul, the Apostle, to the Corinthians,* trans. John Pringle (Grand Rapids: Wm. B. Erdmans Publishing Co., 1948), I, 354.

2. Archibald Robertson and Alfred Plummer, *A Critical and Exegetical Commentary on the First Epistle of St. Paul to the Corinthians* (2d. ed.; Edinburgh: T & T Clark, 1914), p. 229.

3. Louis M. Epstein, *Sex Laws and Customs in Judaism* (New York: Bloch Publishing Co., 1948), p. 40.

4. James Moffatt, *The First Epistle of Paul to the Corinthians* (London: Hodder & Stoughton, 1938), p. 153.

5. Calvin, *op. cit.*, p. 360.

6. Moffatt, *op. cit.*, p. 155.

7. Walter Locke, "A Critical and Exegetical Commentary on the Pastoral Epistles," *The International Critical Commentary* (New York: Charles Scribner's Sons, 1924), XXXVIII, 31.

8. Euripides, *Andromache*, trans. Arthur S. Way (London: William Heinemann, Ltd., 1946), II, 41 f., lines 207-8.

9. John Calvin, *Commentaries on the Epistles of Timothy, Titus, and Philemon,* trans. William Pringle (Grand Rapids: Wm. B. Erdmans Publishing Co., 1948), p. 66.

10. E. F. Scott, *The Pastoral Epistles*, "The Moffatt New Testament Commentary" (London: Hodder & Stoughton, 1948), p. 26.

11. *Ibid.*, p. 28.

Chapter 7

1. P. T. Forsyth, *Marriage: Its Ethic and Religion* (New York and London: Hodder & Stoughton, 1912), p. 70.

2. James S. Stewart, *A Man in Christ* (New York: Harper & Bros., 1935), p. 305. Cf. Romans 15:6; 2 Corinthians 1:3; Colossians 1:3; Ephesians 3:14.

3. Selwyn, *op. cit.*, p. 435.

4. *Ibid.*, p. 182.

5. Elmer G. Homrighausen, "Peter: Exposition," *The Interpreter's Bible* (New York: Abingdon Press, 1957), XII, 121.

6. Bailey, *The Mystery of Love and Marriage, op. cit.*, p. 129.

7. Selwyn, *op. cit.*, p. 184.

8. *Ibid.*, p. 185.

9. *Ibid.*, p. 186.

10. Bailey, *The Mystery of Love and Marriage, op. cit.*, p. 131.

Chapter 8

1. Mace, *op. cit.*, p. 66.

2. Forsyth, *op. cit.*, p. 41.

3. Mace, *op. cit.*, p. 69.

4. *Ibid.*, p. 71.

5. Charles A. Bigg, "A Critical and Exegetical Commentary on the Epistles of St. Peter and St. Jude," *The International Critical Commentary* (Edinburgh: T & T Clark, 1902), pp. 155 f.

6. Mace, *op. cit.*, p. 75.

7. Evelyn Millis Duvall, *In-Laws: Pro and Con* (New York: Association Press, 1954), pp. 89 ff.

8. Mace, *op. cit.*, p. 74.

9. Harry F. Tashman, *The Marriage Bed* (New York: University Publishers, Inc., 1959), pp. 267 ff.

10. Piper, *op. cit.*, p. 130.

11. *Ibid.*

Chapter 9

1. Rudolf Bultmann, *Theology of the New Testament*, trans. Kedrick Grobel (New York: Charles Scribner's Sons, 1954), I, 13 ff.

2. H. E. W. Turner, *Jesus, Master and Lord* (2d. ed.; London: A. R. Mowbray & Co., 1954), p. 306.

3. William Manson, *Jesus, the Messiah* (London: Hodder & Stoughton, Ltd., 1943), p. 82.

4. T. W. Manson, *The Teaching of Jesus* (Cambridge: University Press, 1951), p. 286.

5. *Ibid.*, p. 88.

6. George S. Duncan, *Jesus, Son of Man* (London: Nisbet & Co., Ltd., 1948), p. 219.

7. John A. Broadus, *Commentary on the Gospel of Mark* (Philadelphia: American Baptist Publication Society, 1905), p. 78.

8. Kirsopp Lake, "The Earliest Teaching on Divorce," *The Expositor*, Ser. 7, X (1910), 420.

9. W. C. Allen, *The Gospel According to Saint Mark with Introduction and Notes* (New York: The Macmillan Co., 1915), p. 132.

10. Henry Barclay Swete, *The Gospel According to St. Mark: the Greek Text with Introduction, Notes, and Indices* (London: The Macmillan Co., 1905), p. 216.

11. Vincent Taylor, *The Gospel According to St. Mark* (London: The Macmillan Co., 1952), p. 419.

12. Manson, *The Sayings of Jesus* (London: S. C. M. Press, Ltd., 1949), p. 137.

13. E. Lyttelton, "The Teaching of Christ About Divorce," *Journal of Theological Studies*, V (July, 1904), 623 ff.

14. Bruce Vawter, "The Divorce Clauses in Matthew 5:32 and 19:9," *Catholic Biblical Quarterly*, XVI (1954), 161 ff.

15. R. H. Charles, *The Teaching of the New Testament on Divorce* (London: Williams & Norgate, 1921), p. 11.

16. Bayard H. Jones, "Marriage and Divorce," *Anglican Theological Review*, XXIV (January, 1942), 44.

17. J. P. Arendzen, "Ante-Nicene Interpretations of the Sayings on Divorce," *Journal of Theological Studies*, XX (1918-19), 241.

Chapter 10

1. Robertson and Plummer, *op. cit.*, p. 141.

2. H. E. W. Turner, *Jesus, Master and Lord* (2d. ed.; London: A. R. Mowbray & Co., 1954), p. 337.

3. L. H. Marshall, *The Challenge of New Testament Ethics* (London: The Macmillan Co., 1946), pp. 145 f.

4. Martin Dibelius, *Jesus*, trans. Charles B. Hedrick and F. C. Grant (Philadelphia: The Westminster Press, 1949), p. 116.

5. Augustine, *Commentary on the Lord's Sermon on the Mount with Seventeen Related Sermons*, trans. Denis J. Kavanagh, "The Fathers of the Church" (New York: Fathers of the Church, Inc., 1951), II, 63.

6. Origen, "Commentary on Matthew," *The Ante-Nicene Fathers* (New York: Charles Scribner's Sons, 1899), IX, 511.

7. Mace, *op. cit.*, p. 69.

Chapter 11

1. Charles, *op. cit.*, p. 33.

2. Alan Hugh McNeile, *The Gospel According to St. Matthew* (London: The Macmillan Co., 1949), p. 274.

3. Lyttelton, *op. cit.*, p. 626.

4. See A. T. Cadoux, *The Sources of the Second Gospel* (London: James Clarke & Co., Ltd., 1933), p. 133.

5. McNeile, *op. cit.*, p. 66.

6. Lyttelton, *op. cit.*, p. 623.

7. Charles, *op. cit.*, p. 58.

8. *Ibid.*

9. Arendzen, *op. cit.*

10. N. P. Howington, "The Historic Attitude of the Christian Churches Concerning Marriage, Divorce, and Remarriage" (Thesis, Southern Baptist Theological Seminary, Louisville, Ky., 1948), pp. 114 ff.

11. See *The Ante-Nicene Fathers, op. cit.*, II, 21.

12. Athenagoras, "A Plea for Christians," *ibid.*, 147.

13. Tertullian, "On Monogamy," *ibid.*, IV, 66.

14. ————, "On the Veiling of Virgins," *ibid.*, 33.

15. R. Hugh Connolly (ed.), *Didascalia Apostolorum: The Syriac Version* (Oxford: The Clarendon Press, 1929), XXX, 130.

Chapter 12

1. Maurice Goguel, *The Life of Jesus*, trans. Olive Wyon (New York: The Macmillan Co., 1933), p. 581. Cf. H. E. W. Turner, *op. cit.*, p. 306.

2. Cole, *op. cit.*, p. 121.

3. Piper, *op. cit.*, p. 111.

4. Joseph Fletcher, *Morals and Medicine* (Princeton, N. J.: Princeton University Press, 1954), p. 78.

5. Piper, *op. cit.*, p. 15.

6. See Elias Andrews, *The Meaning of Christ for Paul* (New York: Abingdon Press, 1946), p. 79.

7. Enslin, *op. cit.*, p. 170.

8. H. Chadwick, "All Things to All Men," *New Testament Studies* (1954-55), I, 264.

9. Robertson and Plummer, *op. cit.*, p. 132.

10. Charles Hodge, *An Exposition of the First Epistle to the Corinthians* (New York: A. C. Armstrong & Son, 1894), p. 110.

11. *Ibid.*, p. 113.

12. *Ibid.*, p. 115.

13. Charles, *op. cit.*, pp. 57,59.

14. Richard Crugleman, "1 Corinthians 7:36-38," *The Catholic Biblical Quarterly*, X (1948), 63-70.